101 SICILIAN RECIPES

Sebastiano Accaputo

101 Sicilian Recipes

History, Legends, And Food From Sicily

Sebastiano Accaputo

To my wife Maria and my daughters Giulia and Chiara, whose support has been very important to achieve this result.

TABLE OF CONTENTS

Tournament of the Maiorchino cheese in Novara di Sicilia

PREFACE

Whenever people ask me if I am Italian, I proudly reply "Well, I am Sicilian, something similar but not actually the same."

Because of the age-old architectural, gastronomic, and rich cultural history, Sicilians have long considered themselves as Sicilians way before Italians. Sicilians have our very own flag, a Parliament in Palermo which is considered one of Europe's most ancient. We also take pride in our very own language, for Sicilian is far from being just a dialect.

I am very proud to be part of the Sicilian heritage, and this pride is the reason why I've decided to share with you the recipes most treasured by my own Sicilian family, which best represent the original cuisine of Sicily.

Additionally, I am pleased to recount some of the most common myths and legends that highlight the island's prominent role in the Mediterranean area. The rich historical and cultural background, the stunning landscapes, the unique cuisine, and the mild weather collectively make Sicily one of the most desirable tourist destinations in the Mediterranean Sea.

What Makes Sicilian Recipes Exceptional

Recipes from Sicily are actually some of the world's most singled-out cuisines and this comes with a perfectly good reason. Due to the cultural heritage that is a mixture of several cultures, Sicilian cookery has been formed from many sources, offering assorted recipes intertwined with our very own ingredients.

Sicilian recipes were created from influences of the races which have conquered our land and when they left, they also left behind traces of their own cuisines. From Greeks to Romans, the Arabs, Angevins, Normans,

Spanish, Hapsburgs, Bourbons and the Italians, of course, the Sicilian cookery has turned out to be something that you should not miss trying.

Aside from the diverse cultural influences, the lands of Sicily also have natural resources to die for. Its fertile soil and warm climate also allow the inclusion of varied vegetables and fruits while the seas that surround it abound with plenty of seafood ingredients that are perfect for the most mouthwatering Sicilian dishes.

Most of the traditional Sicilian recipes are products of its bountiful seas, made from sardines, tuna, sepia or cuttlefish, swordfish as well as calamari or squid. Same great samples of Sicilian recipes are Sicilian seared tuna, spicy seafood and the Sicilian stuffed squid.

Meanwhile, Sicily's signature dish makes use of the eggplant, which is known as Caponata. In this regard, it is worth noting that Caponata, as well as Sarde alla Beccafico and many other recipes, stem from the habit of changing ingredients with others that are more economically affordable. The people used to copy the recipes of the nobles but would change the ingredients, and this habit of 'substitution' is a recurring theme in Sicilian culinary tradition.

Sicilians also love rice balls and they have many variations for this certain recipe. Sicilians are famous for their delicious desserts, such as the cassata, a one-of-a-kind cake. It is traditionally made using marzipan, sheep ricotta and candied fruit, making it a real delight.

I am sure that you will also enjoy these original and easy dishes. Who knows, this can already pave the way for you to be famous among your relatives and friends.

Why Try My Sicilian Recipes?

i. These are all traditional recipes that were handed down to me by my own relatives and friends. These recipes represent a true picture of what Sicilians are preparing daily for their families.

ii. Your cookery will definitely be improved when you follow these recipes.

iii. You will surely be popular among your circle of friends.

iv. The ingredients used for these recipes can be bought anywhere and are very affordable.

v. These are not just sumptuous recipes, but they are also very healthy foods that you and your family will love.

Sicilian Flag

Sicilian cuisine is essentially agricultural and maritime: simple but genuine, with thousands of different nuances. Centuries of domination by various populations have enriched the range of typical local dishes with new ingredients and flavours.

Sicilian civilization is unique and has preserved its particular features over the years. It is no coincidence that pasta was born in Sicily, along with sweet and sour sauces (agrodolce), "cassata," stuffed meat, and a wide range of stewed vegetables. Furthermore, many delicacies were imported from the Middle East and Spain, bringing with them the cultural heritage of their origin countries.

The island has a unique environment with volcanoes, a mild climate, the sea, abundant fertile soil, sloping hills, tablelands, and vast plains where a wide range of crops is grown. Sicily is famous worldwide for its delicious ice creams (gelati) made with luscious fruits available throughout the year. Even the frugal meals of the peasant feature a whole series of spicy, attractive dishes.

The ingredients are always wholesome – 'semola' flour, wild vegetables, freshly picked herbs, eggs, and cheese. And, of course, exclusively, extra virgin olive oil is used to make pies, 'mpanate,' and all kinds of fritters.

As islanders, we have our own way of making the various local dishes, using ancient recipes handed down by our grandmas, moms, and aunts. The following recipes have been passed on to me in the same way. The result is a rich variety, thanks also to the influence of the various invaders, which has no equals elsewhere.

The origin of Sicilian cuisine dates back thousands of years, with mentions by Plato, Athenaeus, Pliny, Cicero*, Apicius, and Horace. The Moors, who dominated the island for two hundred years, brought rice and probably pasta, and introduced citrus fruits, exotic spices, cheese, and cane sugar.

*Cicero about cannoli, 70BC: "*Tubus farinarius dulcissimo edulio ex lacte fartus*", that is a tube of flour filled with soft cream of milk.

Many dishes date back to that period, including 'arancini', the famous rice timbales, sweet rice fritters, 'cassata,' 'cannoli,' and even sorbet, thought to derive from the Arab word 'sharbat.' The Spanish, who brought peppers, tomatoes, and potatoes from the Americas, also introduced many dishes along with customs linked to gastronomy: the grand religious festivals, wedding parties, the gaiety of banquets, and Baroque decorations, especially on cakes.

The Bourbons spread the Neapolitan tradition of cooking. At that time, the great families imported their chefs from France, calling them 'monsù,' derived from the French 'monsieur.' These lively characters invented most modern Sicilian dishes, including elaborate preparations such as the sumptuous timbales described in 'Il Gattopardo' written by Tomasi di Lampedusa and in 'The Leopard' directed by Luchino Visconti.

The great travellers of the eighteenth century, captivated by the beauty of the island, did not neglect to highlight the local delicacies. The most famous among them, Goethe, left us with evocative memories of 'cavateddi' made by shy young girls and poetic descriptions of the countryside.

The main motif of Sicilian cuisine is tradition, genuine ingredients, and simplicity—a heritage dictated by the very essence of the Sicilian character, a treasure to be protected and preserved.

AGRIGENTO

The cuisine typical of the Agrigento area was born in the shade of the grand Valley of the Temples, and certainly traces its origins back to the splendid Greek and Roman eras, reflecting the agricultural vocation of the islanders. Pasta is served with simple but genuine sauces such as 'carrittera' sauce. Slightly more elaborate dishes include 'spaghetti alla Pirandello' (see page 53), named after the famous local novelist who won the Nobel Prize for Literature. The wines are exceptional: the province produces a wide variety, and in recent years, vine-growing has replaced the cultivation of vegetables. The grapes, mostly white, ranging from the 'Catarratto' variety to 'Inzolia,' give the wine a fragrant and pleasurable taste. A real treasure is a white wine made from Grillo grapes, a slightly sparkling wine worthy of accompanying the most refined haute cuisine.

CALTANISSETTA

As in the rest of central and southern Sicily, the dishes in the Caltanissetta area are simple but come from a spontaneous tradition of healthy, natural ingredients. The immense wheat fields have given rise to several dishes, including the tasty 'cavateddi.' A typical dish is the 'fuate,' pizzas cooked in stone ovens and often topped with just anchovies and onions. Soups made with potatoes and peppers are also delicious. Broccoli is often cooked with garlic and tomatoes and served with homemade pasta. Boiled tripe is often served with a little oil and a pile of salt heaped in a corner of the plate to dip the pieces of tripe in. The most popular sweet is nougat made with honey, hazelnuts, almonds, and pistachio nuts.

CATANIA

In the Catania area, you will find magnificent creations—tasty, though usually simple recipes made with genuine natural ingredients, always a delight to the palate. They range from 'pasta alla Norma,' named after the opera composed by Vincenzo Bellini, to 'cannelloni,' 'falso magro' (fassumauru), and 'liatina' (pork in jelly). Delights from the rotisserie include rice fritters with anchovies or ricotta, 'staccato' or 'mpanate' (pies with all kinds of fillings), and rice 'arancini.' Etna, the much-loved and hated majestic volcano dominating the panorama, from which precious water flows down to enrich the fertile soil, gives the area treasures such as olives from Biancavilla or the world-renowned pistachio nuts from Bronte. The Etna wines—red, white, and rosé—are full of the strength and generosity of the lava fields. Desserts are highly imaginative, from honey and almond cakes, marzipan fruits, cannoli to Sant'Agata Olives, buns made with honey and dried fruit, and ice creams of all kinds.

ENNA

Among the legends of Ceres and Proserpine, in the shade of ancient castles, you can find a cuisine closely linked to the great wood estates, to the fertile marshlands where wild vegetables and verdant pastures provide the ingredients for genuine, simple but succulent dishes. The pizzas, called 'fuate' in the local language, are topped with oil and pecorino cheese or sizzling bacon fat and baked in a corner of the oven beside the glowing charcoal, which adds extra flavour to them. The local bread deserves a separate mention. In Valguarnera and other towns, special loaves are baked on St. Joseph's Day. They are imaginatively decorated, each loaf becoming a masterpiece of sculpture. Baked in stone ovens and decorated with poppy seeds, its fragrance is heavenly.

Cuddure di San Giuseppe – San Joseph bread

MESSINA

Messina is a noble town stretching out over the straits towards the mainland. From Taormina to Ali, Patti, Tindari, and Capo d'Orlando, you can find a whole parade of succulent dishes in which fish is the main ingredient. The most famous local specialty is swordfish, braised, steamed, roasted in slices, or coated in breadcrumbs. The locally baked leg of pig and sausages from the Peloritan mountains are also famous throughout the island. Artichokes, flans, eggplant balls and roulades, and peppers stuffed with breadcrumbs and olives embellish the endless display of colourful antipasti. The Aeolian Islands are a real paradise for underwater fishing and make a tasty contribution to the pleasure of Messina cuisine.

PALERMO

The gastronomic specialty of the regal, baroque city of Palermo is pasta with a fresh pilchard sauce, whose wealth of colour, variety of ingredients, and exquisite blend of aromas make it a real masterpiece. The 'Vucciria,' the colourful market of the island's capital, is perhaps the best example of how the bright colours of its meat and vegetables, the aromas, and the freshness of the wares artistically displayed on the stalls can be combined to create the most appetizing meals. The surrounding hills and valleys provide a large number of fine wines, in heated rivalry with the nearby province of Trapani. There are a lot of typical desserts, of various historical and traditional origins such as the sumptuous 'cassata,' the 'cannoli' filled with ricotta, and the brightly coloured marzipan fruits.

RAGUSA

The province of Ragusa welcomes visitors with a vast expanse of luxuriant vegetation: hothouses and almond groves, fields of vegetable crops, and olive groves. It is also here, on a vast stretch of land around Vittoria, that grapes for the 'Cerasuolo' wine are grown. With its delicate hint of cherry, it is considered one of the best Sicilian wines, full-bodied and strong.

Mention must also be made of the extraordinary variety of local cheeses: pecorino, fragrant provola, and the famous caciocavallo, which is even cooked in tomato sauce or added to 'mpanate or 'scacciate.'

SIRACUSA

Siracusa's cooking was famous even in Greek times. After a journey on the island, Archestratus wrote a delightful description of the local dishes, and even Plato spoke of the famous banquets held in the city of Ortigia. The Ionian Sea, which the town and the surrounding coastline overlook, is the main source of inspiration, providing the ingredients for numerous fish recipes, including fresh tuna cooked in tomatoes and vinegar, steamed swordfish slices, and the delicious 'Scoppularicchi,' a golden crunchy mixture of fried squid and tiny cuttlefish. Homemade pasta, especially maccheroni made by hand with special tools, blends well with unusual sauces based on walnuts, pine nuts, and olives. A popular wholesome dish is the delicious 'Pasta 'cca muddica'. The excellent wines produced here— Eloro, full-bodied Nero D'Avola in Pachino, and muscatels in Siracusa and Noto—are a fine accompaniment to both savoury and sweet dishes. The almonds from Avola, much sought-after, are used in a variety of extremely refined dessert recipes. Almond 'bianco mangiare' is the best example of a masterpiece of elegance.

TRAPANI

Trapani gastronomy reveals a world of imaginative, unusual recipes, where simple tradition is mixed with ancient history. The various foreign dominations and the traditional agricultural and maritime vocation of the highlanders meet here to give the most wonderful results. Couscous is the prince of local recipes: originally an Arab dish, it is served here with fish and is undoubtedly the most popular of local specialties. Due to the importance of the port and the province's long coastline, fish takes a prominent place among the local recipes. The wines should have a chapter to themselves: the vast stretches of sun-baked land in the area are particularly suited to vine growing, and the local production has its roots in the most ancient winemaking tradition, among the most important in the world. Everyone has heard of the various types of fragrant Marsala, whether sweet or dry, the famous Alcamo whites, and the Pantelleria muscatel made with Zibibbo grapes.

Modica – San Giorgio church

Starters

Panelle

(Chickpea Pancakes)

Panelle are a popular street food in Palermo. Freshly fried panelle are delicious served in a bun (pane e panelle).

Ingredients: (serves 4):

1 litre water, 350 g chickpea flour, 1 bunch of parsley finely chopped, 2 tbsp extra virgin olive oil, seed oil for frying, salt, black pepper.

1. Dissolve the chickpea flour in salted, warm water, stirring lightly to avoid lumps. Place the saucepan over the heat, add the parsley, pepper, and olive oil, and whisk constantly as the batter slowly heats until it starts to thicken.
2. Using a wooden spoon or spatula, spread a small amount of the mixture on a platter or plate, creating a thin layer of 1.5 cm.
3. When the mixture has cooled down, remove and cut into small triangle shapes of 6-7 cm sides.
4. To fry the panelle, pour enough vegetable oil into a heavy skillet to cover the bottom with 1/8 inch of oil and set over medium heat. When the oil is hot, lay the panelle, leaving plenty of space between them.
5. Fry for about 3 minutes until the underside is crisp and golden, then flip them over and brown the second side for about 2 minutes more.
6. Set the panelle on paper towels to drain and cool for a minute, but serve while they are still warm (though they taste good at room temperature too!).

Notes:

_____

_____

_____

_____

_____

_____

Crocchetti 'ri patati

(Potatoes Croquettes)

Ingredients (serves 4 to 6):

1 kg potatoes, 3 tbsp grated pecorino or parmesan cheese, breadcrumbs, 2 eggs, parsley, salt, pepper.

Preparation:

1. In salted water, boil 2 pounds of potatoes with the skin on until tender. Peel and mash with a masher.
2. Add the grated cheese, salt, and pepper to taste, and some finely chopped parsley.
3. Mix well the ingredients to obtain a homogeneous mixture.
4. To make croquettes, wet your hands in oil, pick up a small amount of the mixture, make a small ball, and shape it into the form of a finger.
5. Lightly dredge each croquette first in the whisked eggs and then in the breadcrumbs.
6. To fry the croquettes, use a deep pan, pouring enough oil to cover the croquettes (at least 2 inches deep). Fry croquettes at 200 C degrees until golden brown.

Notes:

_____

_____

_____

_____

_____

_____

15

Myths and Legends

Acis and Galatea (Catania)

Many towns in Sicily are called Aci: Acitrezza, Acireale, Acicastello, Acibonaccorsi, Acicatena, Aci San Flippo, etc.

The poet Ovid, in his "Metamorphoses," tells us the story of love between the beautiful shepherd Aci, son of the Italic god Faunus, and the nymph Symethis, and the nymph Galatea (whose skin is as white as milk), one of the Nereids, sea nymphs daughters of Doris and Nereus.

Aci lived near the volcano Etna, where the Cyclops Polyphemus, who was madly in love with Galatea, also resided.

One day, while Aci was grazing his sheep near the sea, he met Galatea and fell in love with her. Galatea, impressed by the beauty of the young man, reciprocated the feeling.

One evening, in the moonlight, the two were seen kissing on the seashore by Polyphemus, who, mad with jealousy, decided to seek revenge. As soon as Galatea dove into the sea, the giant hurled a lava boulder at Aci, crushing him.

Upon hearing the news, the nymph rushed to her poor beloved and wept inconsolably over his mangled body. Galatea's endless mourning moved the gods, who transformed Aci into a river that originates on the Etna volcano and flows to the point where the two lovers used to meet.

To this day, near Capo Mulini, near the sea in the province of Catania, in a spring with a reddish colour called "u sangu di Jaci" (the blood of Aci), the river Aci concludes its course.

"Son of a Faun and a nymph of the Symethus, Aci was the joy of his father and mother, and even more so mine: he had bound himself exclusively to me. He was beautiful, had just turned sixteen, with tender cheeks barely covered by a faint fuzz. I desired nothing but him, and the Cyclops pursued me relentlessly."

—*OVID, Metamorphoses, Book XIII*

Galatea and Acis found out by Polyphemus the Cyclops, statue in the Jardin du Luxembourg, at the Médicis Fountain. Sculptor: Auguste Ottin.

Pummaroru Cini

(Stuffed Tomatoes)

Ingredients (serves 4):

4 large tomatoes, extra virgin olive oil, 1 onion, 4 salted anchovies, 100 g breadcrumbs, 60 g grated parmesan or pecorino cheese, 1 tbsp capers, 60 g pitted green olives, parsley, basil, extra virgin olive oil (for drizzling).

Preparation:

1. Cut a round slice from the top of the tomatoes to be used later as a lid. With a scoop, scrape out the flesh of the tomato, being careful not to break the skin. Set aside the pulp and the juice.
2. Sauté chopped onion with olive oil for about 3 minutes. Add the anchovies and mash them with a wooden spoon.
3. Add the breadcrumbs and turn them continuously until they are lightly toasted. Remove from flame and set aside to cool.
4. Chop the pulp and mix it with juice. In a bowl, combine the pulp and juice with the cooled breadcrumb mixture, add the cheese, parsley, basil, capers, olives, salt, and pepper to taste.
5. Sprinkle salt inside the hollow tomatoes, and equally fill the tomatoes. Cover with lids, and arrange in a greased baking dish, standing the stuffed tomatoes with the lid side up.
6. Drizzle with 2 tablespoons of olive oil and bake at 180° C for 45 minutes.

Notes:

_____

_____

_____

_____

_____

_____

Ova Cini

(Stuffed Eggs)

Excellent as an antipasto or, during summer as a dish served with fresh tomato salad.

Ingredients (serves four):

6 eggs, 2 salted anchovies, 170 g tuna in olive oil, capers, olive oil.

Preparation:

1. Hard-boil six eggs, shell, cut in half in the length, and remove the yolk.
2. Put the yolks together and add the cleaned and chopped anchovies, the tuna, and chopped capers. Mix the compound with a bit of olive oil until they have become a cream.
3. Stuff the albumens.
4. Place the half eggs on a plate and decorate with leaves of green salad.

Notes:

_____

_____

_____

_____

_____

_____

Fave Vugghiuti 'a Sarausana

(Siracusan style boiled broad beans)

Ingredients (serves 4):

500g dry broad beans, 5 garlic cloves, extra virgin olive oil, salt, black pepper.

Preparation:

1. Rinse the dry broad beans and place them in a large saucepot with abundant water. Soak overnight.
2. Using a knife, eliminate the dark membrane on top of each bean.
3. Rinse the beans and place them with the garlic in a saucepot with salted water. Bring to a boil and lower the heat, simmer for 2 hours.
4. When ready, drain the extra liquid and transfer into a serving dish.
5. Dress broad beans with extra virgin olive oil, salt, and pepper to taste, and serve hot or cold.
6. As an option, it is possible to add a tbsp of fresh ricotta cheese.

Notes:

_____

_____

_____

_____

_____

_____

Pani Cunzatu abbruscatu

(Bruschetta)

Bruschetta is the most common and easy antipasto that is prepared in my family because it is quick to prepare and delicious. It is sliced Italian bread rubbed with fresh garlic, drizzled with olive oil, sprinkled with salt, placed on an oven rack and toasted until golden and lightly crispy.

Ingredients (serves 6):

1 loaf of Italian bread, 2 garlic cloves, extra virgin olive oil, 1 small red onion, tomatoes, salt, black pepper.

Preparation:

1. Preheat oven to 180 C degrees.
2. Slice bread (about 1.5 cm) into 20 to 24 pieces.
3. Rub each slice with garlic and brush with olive oil.
4. Place slices in a baking pan and toast until golden, 5 to 8 minutes.
5. Separately, mix in a bowl 250 g diced tomato, ½ small red onion, 2 tbsp of olive oil, oregano, salt, and pepper.
6. Place this topping over the bread, drizzle with remaining oil, and sprinkle with salt and pepper.
7. Serve hot.

Notes:

_____

_____

_____

_____

_____

_____

Iammuru cunzatu

(Marinated prawns)

Ingredients (serves 4):

400 g whole fresh prawns, 4 lemons, 2 bunches of feathery fennel leaves, fresh mint and fresh parsley, 2 garlic cloves, coarse salt, pepper, extra virgin olive oil.

Preparation:

1. Wash and shell the prawns. Clean your hands by rubbing them with half a lemon.
2. Grate the zest from the lemons and set it aside. Squeeze the lemons and crush the garlic cloves on a plate.
3. Place the prawns on the plate with the lemon juice and garlic, and let them marinate in the fridge for about 5 hours.
4. Drain the prawns well, remove the garlic, and add the parsley and fennel leaves. Sauté in a bowl and add a pinch of coarse salt, the lemon zest, and some extra virgin olive oil.
5. Serve on a plate over a bed of rocket leaves.

Notes:

_____

_____

_____

_____

_____

_____

Capunata ri Milinciani

(Eggplants Caponata)

This is a typical Sicilian dish based on vegetables, primarily on eggplants. The word "caponata" seems to come from the fish "capone," which is the way the dolphinfish is called in Sicily—a fish with delicious but quite dry meat. It used to be served in the dining tables of Sicilian aristocracy dressed with a sweet-and-sour sauce that characterizes caponata. The people, unable to afford the cost of the fine fish, replaced it with economical eggplants. This is the recipe that has been handed down to date. This dish, served cold as an antipasto, is very popular all over Italy. It can be eaten warm as an accompaniment to meat and poultry or used as a pasta dressing.

Ingredients (serves 4):

4 eggplants, 2 white diced onions, 2 celery stalks, 50 g green pitted olives, 30 g capers, 3 red peppers, ½ glass white vinegar, 1 tbsp sugar, 1 tbsp double-concentrated tomato, salt, mint, extra virgin olive oil.

Preparation:

1. Coarsely dice the eggplants, sprinkle them with salt, and let them rest for half an hour in a colander to remove the bitter liquid. Wash and dry, then fry the eggplants in abundant hot oil and set aside.
2. Separately fry onion, celery, and diced pepper. Add green pitted olives, washed capers, and some leaves of mint.
3. Add the double-concentrated tomato, salt, and sugar, stir in the white vinegar, and cook until it evaporates.
4. Now, add the fried eggplants, correct the salt, and cook for a further 10 minutes (a bit of hot water can be used to correct the density of the mixture).

5. Serve the caponata cold.

Notes:

_____

_____

_____

_____

_____

_____

Saltern, Trapani

Cacocciuli cini

(Stuffed artichokes)

Ingredients (serves 4):

4 artichokes, 120 g breadcrumbs, 2 garlic cloves, extra virgin olive oil, parsley, salt, pepper.

Preparation:

1. Wash the artichokes and prepare them by cutting off the stems and removing any tough outer leaves.
2. Holding them upside down, strike against a table surface to make the leaves open easily.
3. Mix the breadcrumbs with salt, pepper, garlic, and parsley.
4. Using a teaspoon, stuff the artichokes, pressing down the mixture between the layers of leaves, starting from the external ones.
5. Place them standing up in a casserole with a small amount of water and pour some olive oil over each one.
6. Cover and cook on low heat for at least half an hour.

Notes:

_____

_____

_____

_____

_____

_____

Cacocciuli 'a campagnola

(Country style artichokes)

Ingredients (serves 6):

6 artichokes, 3 garlic cloves, 2 anchovy fillets, grated pecorino or parmesan cheese, parsley, mint leaves, extra virgin olive oil, 2 tbsp breadcrumbs, salt, pepper, ½ lemon.

Preparation:

1. Prepare a basin with water and the juice of half a lemon to soak the artichokes after trimming to prevent discoloration.
2. Remove the stems and discard hard outer leaves until the artichoke's leaves become light in colour and tender.
3. Cut the artichokes in half lengthwise, eliminate any prickly leaves, and remove the non-edible part inside.
4. Place the cut artichokes in a pot with lightly salted cold water; add a few drops of lemon juice.
5. Bring the pot to a boil and simmer for 20/30 minutes, checking frequently and adding water if needed. When cooked, set aside.
6. In a medium-sized skillet, sauté the minced garlic in olive oil. Remove from heat and add the anchovies, stirring until they dissolve. Set aside.
7. In the same skillet, lightly toast the breadcrumbs with 1 tablespoon of olive oil and set aside.
8. Place the artichokes in an oiled baking pan, sprinkle each with salt and pepper to taste.

9. Divide equally on top of the halved artichokes the cheese, remaining parsley, mint, sautéed garlic and anchovies, and dust with lightly toasted breadcrumbs.

10. Bake at 200°C for 15 minutes. Serve hot or cold.

Notes:

_____

_____

_____

_____

_____

_____

Myths and Legends

Scylla and Charybdis (Messina)

Scylla and Charybdis lived on opposite sides of the narrow Strait of Messina, situated between Italy and Sicily. The legend originated to explain the whirlpools and the turbulent sea that claimed the lives of sailors in ancient times.

Once upon a time in Calabria, there lived a beautiful girl named Scilla. Glauco, the son of Poseidon, fell in love with her, but Circe the Sorceress also harboured affection for the boy. Fuelled by jealousy, Circe cast a spell against Scilla. When Scilla touched the water, she transformed into a horrific sea monster with six dog heads and twelve tentacle-like legs, which dragged her away, destroying the land between Italy and Sicily in their frenzied race, creating an island. Since then, Scilla, confined in a cave, devours sailors stranded on the rocks.

On the opposite side of the straight, Charybdis (in Sicilian dialect Cariddi), too, was a beautiful girl living in Messina, but she was insatiably voracious. Unfortunately, one day, she devoured Jupiter's sacred cattle. As punishment, the god threw her off a cliff and condemned her to swallow the seawater, causing the whirlpools in which unfortunate sailors met their demise.

The phrase "between Scylla and Charybdis" has come to symbolize being in a situation where one is between two dangers, and moving away from one will expose them to danger from the other.

Scylla. (From a coin of Agrigentum.)

Giardini Naxos, Messina

Vrocculi friuti

(Fried broccoli)

Ingredients (serves 4):

600 g of broccoli, 4 garlic cloves, dried tomatoes, extra virgin olive oil, red chili peppers, salt and pepper.

Preparation:

1. Cut and discard 2 cm from the base of the broccoli. Separate florets from the stalks and cut the florets to keep them the same size.
2. Peel the tough outer membrane of the stalks and cut them into slices or wedges, then set aside.
3. Bring a large pot of salted water to a boil and place the broccoli stalks in it. Cook for 3 minutes. Add the florets and continue cooking for 6 minutes, starting from the time it boils again.
4. Using a slotted spoon, place the broccoli in a container and set aside.
5. When ready to serve, brown the crushed garlic in a pan with olive oil over medium heat. When the garlic turns golden in colour, remove the pan from the fire, add the broccoli, and place it again over medium heat, stirring for a couple of minutes.
6. Taste for salt, add a pinch of chili pepper and black pepper to taste.
7. Place the broccoli on a serving plate and pour the oil and garlic on top. Serve the broccoli with hot crusty bread to dip into the juice.

Notes:

_____

_____

_____

_____

_____

_____

Masculinu cunzatu

(Marinated anchovies)

Ingredients (serves 4):

1 kg fresh anchovies, 500 ml white wine vinegar, juice of 1 lemon, extra virgin olive oil, 2 tbsp dried oregano, 2 tbsp hot red pepper flakes, 30 g finely chopped parsley, 4 garlic cloves, sliced paper-thin, 2 tablespoons sea salt, lemon wedges (optional).

Preparation:

1. Clean the anchovies by cutting off the heads and carefully pull out the spine and pin bones with your index finger and thumbnail. Separate the two fillets and rinse again.
2. Arrange a layer of the fillets in a deep oval gratin dish, and sprinkle with a tablespoon or two of vinegar. Continue until all the fish fillets are used, then pour the rest of the vinegar and the lemon juice over the fish. Cover and marinate in the fridge for at least 4 hours.
3. Remove the anchovies from the vinegar, rinse, and pat dry with a kitchen towel. Wash out the dish and dry well.
4. Return a single layer of cured anchovies to the dish and sprinkle with 2 or 3 tablespoons olive oil, a pinch of oregano, a pinch of pepper flakes, a pinch of parsley, three or four garlic slices, and a pinch of salt.
5. Layer in the rest of the anchovies, sprinkling each layer with oil, oregano, pepper flakes, parsley, garlic, and salt. Cover again and marinate in the fridge for at least 2 hours.
6. Serve anchovies at room temperature.

Notes:

_____

_____

_____

_____

_____

_____

Mulinciani a cutuletta

(Breaded eggplants)

Ingredients:

3 large purple eggplants, salt, 3 large eggs, 1 bunch chopped parsley, 100 g breadcrumbs, freshly ground black pepper, extra virgin olive oil.

Preparation:

1. Slice the eggplants into round slices, each about 2 cm thick.
2. Sprinkle the slices liberally with salt and then place them in a colander. Leave the eggplant in the colander for at least 1 hour, giving the salt time to absorb the eggplant's bitterness. Don't rinse the eggplant, just shake off excess water.
3. When eggplants are ready to be used, beat the three eggs in a shallow bowl. Spread the breadcrumbs out in a baking pan. Season the eggplant slices to taste with salt and pepper.
4. Lightly dredge each eggplant slice first in the egg and then in the breadcrumbs.
5. In a saucepan, heat extra-virgin olive oil over medium heat. When the oil is very hot, lay several eggplant slices in a single layer in the pan.
6. Fry the slices until golden brown, about 2 minutes on each side.
7. When the first batch is cooked, remove the eggplant from the pan to a serving dish using a slotted spoon.
8. Repeat the cooking process until all of the cutlets are cooked.
9. Serve warm.

Notes:

_____

_____

_____

_____

_____

_____

Places & Traditions

Mercato della Vucciria (Palermo)

The markets of Palermo indeed carry the essence of North Africa. After all, Arabs dominated Sicily for two hundred years and many markets, built during that time, resemble the market or *suk* of any Muslim city.

Even today, you can notice the appearance, colours, smells, and the custom of flooding streets and squares with stalls, baskets, and various colourful awnings, typical of traditional North African markets. Particularly characteristic are the habits of selling and buying, where the shouts of the stall vendors calling out to buyers at the top of their lungs and the bargaining over prices or complaints about the exact weight of the merchandise are vivid and colourful. And this is not only in Palermo. I have vivid memories of my mother engaged in endless discussions about the quality of the goods and the requests for a "discount." After all, "lei u sapi, iu clienti sugnu, sempri 'nti lei vegnu e accattu," which means "I always come here to buy," and therefore, I deserve a discount.

The two main markets, La Vucciria and Mercato di Capo, create a vibrant atmosphere. La Vucciria, centred around Piazza San Domenico, extends into the surrounding streets, offering a plethora of fresh fish, meat, and recently harvested delights like wild fennel, artichokes, and blood oranges.

On the other hand, Mercato di Capo, emanating from Chiesa di Sant Agostino, features not only food items but also clothing stalls and leather goods. Of course, the market showcases the staples of fish, meat, fruits, and vegetables.

Wandering through the streets, indulging in panelle or calzoni, is a delightful experience. Vuccirìa stands out as the largest and most popular market street in Palermo, resembling a bustling casbah. It presents a diverse array of food, from fresh swordfish steaks to various meats and recently harvested produce, showcasing the richness of Sicilian countryside offerings. The market is a spectacle with wild fennel, long-stemmed artichokes, blood oranges, and giant octopus.

La Vucciria market operates Monday through Saturday until 2 pm. For the most vibrant and colourful experience, it's recommended to visit before 10 am when the market is at its peak of activity.

Palermo – Vucciria

Parmigiana ri Mulinciani

(Melanzane alla parmigiana)

My family used to prepare this dish, especially during the summer when there are plenty of locally grown fresh eggplants in Sicily. Despite the name (parmigiana could mean made in Parma), this dish originated in Sicily and then spread throughout the country, becoming very popular. The word "parmigiana" seems to be a distortion of the dialectal word "parmiciana," which is a type of shutter, alluding to the way in which the eggplant slices are laid.

Ingredients (serves 4):

4 eggplants, 1 big can of whole peeled tomatoes, grated cheese (in the original version caciocavallo, but parmesan is okay), fresh basil, garlic (for the tomato sauce), extra virgin olive oil, salt.

Preparation:

1. For the tomato sauce, mince garlic cloves into small pieces, fry them in 2 tbsp olive oil, and after ~1 minute, add tomatoes.
2. Keep cooking, covered, for ~20 minutes, then remove the lid and let some water evaporate. Add salt to taste, blend with an immersion blender, and set aside.
3. Cut eggplants lengthwise into slices one cm thick and put them on a plate covered with plenty of salt for about 1 hour.
4. Wash off the excess salt and dry the slices with a paper towel. Fry them in abundant hot oil.
5. When the slices are well coloured, take them out of the pan and put them in a colander to lose the excess oil.

46

6. Pour some tomato sauce onto a large plate and then place the first layer of fried eggplants.
7. Then, place more sauce and add the cheese and some leaves of basil. Place another layer of eggplants and repeat the process.
8. Pour more sauce and a final layer of cheese and some basil. Put in a hot oven for 15-20 minutes. Parmigiana should be served hot.

Notes:

_____

_____

_____

_____

_____

Milinciani arrustuti

(Roasted eggplants)

Ingredients (serves 4):

4 eggplants, 2 garlic cloves, extra virgin olive oil, salt and black pepper, mint, parsley, white vinegar.

Preparation:

1. Slice the eggplants into 1 cm thick slices and grill them.
2. In a bowl, mix olive oil, chopped parsley, chopped mint, chopped garlic, salt, pepper, and vinegar.
3. Place the grilled eggplants in layers with the dressing.

Taormina and Etna with snow

Pipi cini

(Roasted peppers filled)

This is a dish that could be served as an antipasto or second course.

Ingredients:

8 green, yellow, and red peppers, 400 g breadcrumbs (an alternative is boiled rice), 60 g grated pecorino cheese, 2 tbsp pine nuts, 2 tbsp raisins, 4 minced garlic cloves, ½ minced onion, 1 bunch finely chopped parsley, 1 tsp oregano, 1 egg, black pepper, extra virgin olive oil.

Preparation:

1. To make the filling, lightly moisten the breadcrumbs and put them in a large mixing bowl.
2. Add the pecorino cheese, parsley, pine nuts, raisins, garlic, onion, oregano, egg, a pinch of black pepper, and 2 tbsp of olive oil.
3. Mix well for a couple of minutes.
4. Fill each pepper with the stuffing and replace the tops, rub with olive oil, and place them in a baking pan in the preheated oven.
5. Turn the peppers in the tin occasionally and let them cook for about 40 minutes.
6. Remove the peppers from the oven and let them cool.

Notes:

_____

_____

_____

_____

_____

Cozzi gratinati

(Mussels au gratin)

Ingredients (serves 4):

1 kg large mussels, ½ glass white wine, 200 g breadcrumbs, parsley, grated pecorino cheese, oregano, 4 garlic cloves, black pepper, extra virgin olive oil.

Preparation:

1. Wash and scrub the mussels well, and remove the beard.
2. In a bowl, prepare the filling by mixing breadcrumbs, chopped parsley, grated pecorino cheese, oregano, minced garlic, and fresh ground black pepper.
3. Steam the mussels with white wine in a covered pan over high heat until they all open. Optionally, add the zest of a lemon with the raw mussels.
4. Transfer the steamed mussels into a colander, let them drain and cool. Eliminate and discard any empty shells.
5. Preheat the oven to 180°C.
6. Lightly oil a shallow baking pan. Add some of the drained mussel juice to the filling and lightly moisten the mixture.
7. Spoon the filling over each mussel, place them in the baking pan, drizzle with olive oil, and bake in the preheated oven for about 15 minutes or until lightly golden brown.
8. Serve hot with lemon slices.

Notes:

_____

_____

_____

_____

_____

_____

Milinciani cini

(Filled eggplants)

Ingredients (serves 4):

4 small eggplants, 50 g breadcrumbs, 50 g grated cheese, 3 tbsp tomato sauce, 50 g fresh cheese, 2 eggs, 50 g cooked ham, salt, basil, black pepper.

Preparation:

1. Cut the eggplants in half lengthwise and place them in boiling water for about 10 minutes.
2. Using a tablespoon, remove the pulp, leaving a layer of 1 cm inside.
3. Chop the removed pulp and mix it with grated cheese, breadcrumbs, chopped hard-boiled eggs, fresh cheese in cubes, chopped cooked ham, chopped basil leaves, and the sauce.
4. Add some salt and pepper, and mix well.
5. Stuff the empty eggplants and place them with a bit of sauce in an oiled baking tin.
6. Spread with breadcrumbs and grated cheese, and drizzle with a little olive oil.
7. Put in the oven at 180°C for 20 minutes until they have a golden crust.

Notes:

_____

_____

_____

_____

_____

_____

'Nzalata r'aranci

(Salad with oranges)

This is a particularly easy salad that is very appreciated in Sicily and represents one of the most common antipastos during Christmas time. As with a lot of traditional recipes, we have to thank the Arabs who imported the oranges to Sicily in the XII century.

Ingredients (serves 4)

6 oranges, 2 spring onions, olive oil, salt, red chili pepper, olives, anchovies, capers (optional)

Preparation:

1. Peel the oranges (preferably the red ones) and cut into pieces.
2. Add the spring onions, cleaned and chopped.
3. Dress with olive oil, salt, and red chili pepper.

   Optionally, you can add a couple of anchovies or herrings, olives or capers.

Notes:

_____

_____

_____

_____

_____

_____

'Nzalata fummaggiu e pipi

(Salad with cheese and roasted peppers)

Ingredients (serves 4):

250 g fresh cheese (pecorino or 4 small mozzarella balls), 4 large red peppers, basil leaves, 12 cherry tomatoes, extra virgin olive oil, salt, black pepper.

Preparation:

1. Roast the peppers in the oven or directly on the range or grill, turning them until each side has evenly cooked. Place them in a paper or plastic bag and let them cool.
2. Once the peppers are cool enough to handle, peel off the skin and cut off the stems, then slice away the ribs and remove the seeds. Quarter the peppers by slicing them lengthwise.
3. Cut the cheese into 1.5 cm cubes and arrange them on a serving plate, alternating them with the pepper slices and the cherry tomatoes cut in half.
4. Place the basil leaves and drizzle with extra virgin olive oil, salt, and pepper to taste, then serve.

Notes:

_____

_____

_____

_____

_____

_____

Myths and Legends

The rape of Persephone (Enna)

Beautiful Persephone lived a peaceful life until Hades, the Lord of the Underworld, fell in love with her. It is said that Zeus advised him to carry her off, as her mother Demeter was not likely to allow. She was innocently picking flowers with some nymphs in a field when Hades came to abduct her, bursting through a cleft in the earth.

The place where Persephone was said to have been carried off is in the meadows near Enna. Demeter searched desperately with torches for her lost daughter all over the world. In the depths of her despair, she caused nothing to grow on the earth.

Helios, the sun, who saw everything, eventually told Demeter what had happened and at length, she discovered the place of her abode. Finally, Zeus, pressed by the cries of the hungry people and the other deities who also heard their anguish, forced Hades to return Persephone.

However, it was a rule of the Fates that whoever consumed food or drink in the Underworld was doomed to spend eternity there. Before Persephone was released to Hermes, who had been sent to retrieve her, Hades tricked her into eating pomegranate seeds, which forced her to return to the underworld for a period each year.

The seeds correspond to the dry summer months, usually one third of the year (four months) when Persephone is absent. When Demeter and her daughter were reunited, the Earth flourished with vegetation and colour, but for some months each year, when Persephone returned to the underworld, the Earth once again became a barren realm.

This is an origin story to explain the seasons.

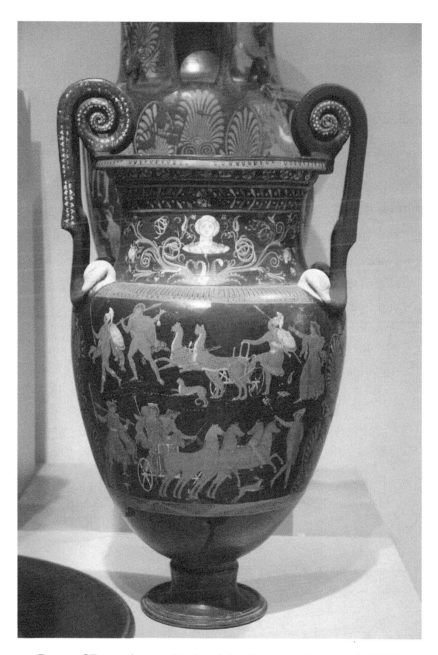

Rape of Persephone, Circle of the Darius painter, c. 340 BC

Patati, ricotta e cipudda

(Potatoes, ricotta cheese and onions)

Ingredients (serves 4)

1 kg potatoes, 2 red onions, ½ kg ricotta cheese, extra virgin olive oil, salt, pepper.

Preparation:

1. Peel the potatoes and cut them into slices of about ½ cm.
2. Place a layer of sliced potatoes and sliced onions in a baking tin, add a layer of ricotta cheese, and then another layer of potatoes and onions.
3. Sprinkle with salt, pepper, and generously drizzle olive oil.
4. Put the tin in the oven preheated to 180°C for 30 minutes or until the potatoes are cooked.

Notes:

_____

_____

_____

_____

_____

_____

Frittata ri patati e cipudda

(Potatoes and onion flan)

Ingredients (serves 4):

3 large potatoes, 2 large onions, 6 large eggs, 1 tbsp capers, 100 g grated parmesan or caciocavallo cheese, salt and black pepper, olive oil.

Preparation:

1. Dice the potatoes into 2 cm cubes, then rinse and dry them with a kitchen towel. Peel and slice the onions into thin rings.
2. In a mixing bowl, whisk the eggs and add the capers, grated parmesan, salt, and freshly ground pepper.
3. Fry the potato cubes in olive oil over moderate heat until they turn lightly golden, then place them on paper towels to absorb any excess oil.
4. Fry the onions until they are translucent.
5. In either a ceramic or glass baking casserole, start by layering potatoes followed by a thin layer of onions.
6. Pour some of the egg mixture on top of the potatoes and onions and repeat the procedure until all of the potatoes and onions are in the baking dish, reserving enough of the egg mixture for the top.
7. Add a little extra grated cheese and place in a preheated oven at 180° C for about 20 to 30 minutes or until the eggs are completely cooked and golden on top.

Notes:

_____

_____

_____

_____

_____

_____

Cucuzzi 'e uova

(Zucchini and eggs)

Ingredients (serves 4):

500 g zucchini, 4 large eggs, 3 tbsp pecorino cheese, 2 tbsp capers, salt and black pepper, olive oil for frying.

Preparation:

1. Clean the zucchini, cut off the ends, and discard them. Slice the zucchini into round 1 cm pieces.
2. Rinse the capers and remove the salt. Whisk the eggs into a bowl. Add a pinch of salt, the grated cheese, the minced capers, and a few twists of ground black pepper.
3. Heat a skillet over moderate heat, add enough olive oil to coat the bottom of the pan, then add the zucchini slices and fry until golden brown on each side.
4. Add more olive oil if necessary and pour in the egg mixture.
5. Cook on a moderate heat, turning from time to time. When the eggs are thoroughly cooked and lightly browned, transfer to a plate and serve warm or cold.
6. Add more grated cheese if desired.

Notes:

_____

_____

_____

_____

_____

_____

Ghiotta ri pipi

(Peperonata)

Ingredients (serves 4):

800 g peppers (green, yellow, and red), 400 g potatoes, 2 onions, 3 ripe tomatoes, olive oil, salt, black pepper.

Preparation:

For optimal results, choose fleshy and sweet peppers.

1. Cut the peppers lengthwise, removing stalks and seeds, and then chop them into large chunks.
2. In a pan, stir-fry peppers and sliced onions with generous olive oil.
3. Add potatoes cut into small pieces.
4. Cover the pan and simmer on low heat for 20 minutes.
5. In another pan, fry peeled tomatoes and incorporate them into the other ingredients. Season with salt and pepper.

Notes:

_____

_____

_____

_____

_____

Sveva Tower – Vendicari, Siracusa

Pink Flamingos – Vendicari, Siracusa

Myths and Legends

The legend of Colapesce (Messina)

Colapesce is one of the most loved and known Sicilian legends in the world. Many American and European poets have written stories based on it.

Colapesce, son of a fisherman, used to spend his days swimming in the sea. One day, his mother tired of his behaviour, cast a spell on him. So, Colapesce became half man and half fish and never returned to the land.

After hearing his story, the King of Sicily wanted to meet him. He went near Messina, where Colapesce lived, and challenged the boy by throwing a golden cup into the waves. Colapesce retrieved it from the submarine abyss and told the king about the marvellous things he had seen.

The king then threw his crown into the sea, and Colapesce retrieved it, revealing that he had seen Sicily supported by three columns. One was collapsing, the other was in bad condition, and only one was good. He also mentioned a magical fire in the abyss. The king didn't believe his report and threw his golden ring into the sea.

Colapesce, although exhausted, dived again, but he told the king he would have shown evidence even if it was extremely dangerous. After some hours, the ring returned, burnt. After a while, a piece of wood also came back, burned too. Colapesce, however, never reemerged.

The legend says that he remained at the bottom of the sea to support the last column. His sacrifice saved Sicily, and that's why Sicilian people love him so much.

Puppetti ri patati

(Potatoes rissoles)

Ingredients (serves 4):

1 kg potatoes, 4-5 eggs, 50 g breadcrumbs, 50 g grated hard cheese, 1 garlic clove, 1 parsley bunch, salt and pepper, olive oil.

Preparation:

1. Boil the potatoes in salted water.
2. Peel them and mash them well.
3. When the mashed potatoes are cold, mix them with the whisked eggs, breadcrumbs, grated cheese, chopped parsley, and crushed garlic. Mix well.
4. Shape the mixture into oval rissoles and fry them in a pan with generous hot oil.

Notes:

_____

_____

_____

_____

_____

_____

Main Courses

Pani Cunzatu

(Seasoned filled loaf)

Driving from Catania to Siracusa, near the junction to Agnone Bagni, on the SS 114, I used to visit a bar/bakery named "Al Pane Condito". Here it was possible to buy a special loaf baked in a wood oven, cut in the middle, and seasoned with abundant olive oil, oregano, chili pepper, and fresh pecorino. The view from this point was breathtaking as you could see the Bay of Catania with the Etna volcano in the background.

Ingredients:

1 loaf of hard grain or whole wheat bread (about 800 g), 400 g of fresh pecorino (sheep milk cheese) or tuma (cow milk cheese), oregano, salt, red chili pepper, extra virgin olive oil.

Preparation:

1. Cut the loaf in the middle and season with a generous pinch of salt, oregano, and chili pepper. Add the oil.
2. Cut the cheese into slices and place them on the seasoned bread.
3. Close the loaf, cut it into four pieces, and consume this way, or put it on a panini grill or in a preheated oven for 5 minutes.
4. A glass of red Nero d'Avola or a beer is recommended.
5. You can add other ingredients to taste, such as slices of fresh tomato, fresh onion, anchovies, sundried tomato, olives, etc.

Notes:

_____

_____

_____

_____

_____

_____

Spaghetti alla Pirandello

(Spaghetti Pirandello style)

Ingredients (serves 6):

600 g bucatini, 100 g black olives, 100 g grated Parmesan cheese, 50 g butter, 30 g capers (desalted), 1 kg ripe tomatoes, 5 tbsp extra virgin olive oil, 2 cloves garlic, 3 anchovy fillets, 1 eggplant, 1 sweet pepper, 1 bunch basil, salt, chili pepper.

Preparation:

1. Cut the eggplant into cubes and brown them in hot oil.
2. Roast the pepper on a hot plate, peel it, remove the seeds, and cut it into strips.
3. Brown the garlic in a pan with olive oil on low heat, then add the anchovies. Mash them with a wooden spoon, and add the capers and pitted olives. Stir for a few minutes.
4. Add the peeled and chopped tomatoes, and basil leaves, and cook for 20 minutes. Add the roasted pepper and cook for another 5 minutes. Remove from heat and add the eggplants.
5. Cook the bucatini in salted boiling water until "al dente," drain well, and place on a serving plate.
6. Mix with half of the dressing sauce, butter, and half of the grated Parmesan. Cover with the remaining sauce and cheese. Mix well and serve.

Luigi Pirandello receives the news of being awarded the Nobel Prize on November 9, 1934. Under the flashes of photographers gathered in his studio at Via Bosio 15, he types: Clowning! Clowning!

Arancini ri risu

(Sicilian Arancini with meat)

This recipe illustrates the procedure to prepare spheric-shaped arancini. The most traditional shape is though conic. But you will usually find on display both shapes as they may contain different fillings such as spinach or ham and cheese.

For the external:

500 g Arborio risotto rice, 50 g butter, 800 ml chicken stock, 1 free-range egg, 80 g grated parmesan.

For the filling:

200 g lean minced beef, a handful of frozen peas, 1 garlic clove, 150 ml tomato puree, 1 tbsp tomato puree, 1 tbsp olive oil, salt and pepper to taste, 10 one-pound-coin-size mozzarella chunks.

For the coating:

300 g breadcrumbs made from real stale bread, 2 free-range eggs, beaten and seasoned.

Preparation:

1. In a deep-bottomed pan, start by melting the butter and add the rice. Fry it gently and then add the hot stock, one ladle at a time, until the risotto is thoroughly cooked. This will take about 30 minutes. Set aside to cool at room temperature and then add the parmesan and egg, mixing with your hands. Now refrigerate the rice for an hour.

2. In the meantime, it's time to make the filling. Heat up the oil in a pan and fry the meat until slightly brown. Then add the garlic and tomato puree, frying for another minute. Now add the puree and peas, season, and let the sauce reduce on low heat for 30 minutes. Set aside to cool.

3. After an hour, take the rice mix out of the fridge and line up all the ingredients on your work service, adding a little bowl of water for you to wet your hands. Wet your hands, pick up some of the rice mixture, and give the rice the shape of a cup. Put a teaspoon of the meat mixture in it, a chunk of the cheese, and cover with some more of the rice. Press lightly and roll it in your hands until you get a nice round ball as big as a small orange and set it aside. You should end up with about 10 of them. Now refrigerate for another 30 minutes to an hour in order for the rice to become firm again.

4. After an hour you are ready to coat your arancini, dipping them in the beaten eggs and covering them in breadcrumbs. Heat some vegetable oil to 180° C in either a deep-fat fryer or medium-size saucepan. Fry the arancini for a few minutes until they are golden brown, and then drain them on kitchen paper to remove the excess oil.

Notes:

_____

_____

_____

_____

_____

_____

Greek theatre, Siracusa

Spaghetti 'cca bottarga ri tunnu

(Spaghetti with roe of tuna)

Ingredients (serves 4)

8 tablespoons extra virgin olive oil, 1 tbsp crushed red pepper, 2 garlic cloves thinly sliced, 400 g spaghetti, 2 bunches parsley finely chopped, 150 g bottarga of tuna, peeler or grater, zest of 2 lemons.

Preparation:

1. Heat 2 litres of water to boil and add 2 tablespoons of salt.
2. In a 30 cm sauté pan, heat olive oil, red pepper, and garlic over low heat until just fragrant, about 2 minutes, and remove from heat.
3. Cook spaghetti according to package instructions until just al dente.
4. Drain and pour into the oil mixture and add parsley. Toss to mix well over medium heat and pour into a warmed serving bowl.
5. Shave Bottarga over the bowl, sprinkle with lemon zest, and serve immediately.

Notes:

_____

_____

_____

_____

_____

_____

Maccarruna 'cco sucu ra sasizza

(Macaroni with sausage sauce)

Ingredients (serves 4):

400 g rigatoni, 400 g sweet pork, Italian-style sausages, 200 g crushed ripe tomatoes, 1 medium onion, 2 garlic cloves, ½ glass red wine, 60 g peas, extra virgin olive oil, salt and pepper.

Preparation:

1. Chop the onions and crumble the sausages.
2. Brown the onion in a large saucepan over moderate heat, add the garlic, and then add the crumbled sausage and cook until it is lightly browned.
3. Turn down the heat to low, pour in the red wine and, after a couple of minutes, add the tomatoes, cover, and simmer.
4. Add the peas, remove the sauce from the hob, and set aside.
5. Cook the pasta al dente, strain and immediately toss in the pan with the sauce.
6. Return the pan to the hob and, over moderate heat, stir together the pasta and sauce until evenly combined and hot.
7. Serve with grated caciocavallo or pecorino cheese.

Notes:

_____

_____

_____

_____

_____

_____

'Nzalata ri pasta

(Pasta salad)

Ingredients (serves 4):

500g ridged penne or fusilli, 4 garlic cloves, 16 ripe cherry tomatoes, 4 fresh mozzarella balls, basil leaves, 2 tbsp capers, pitted olives, chilli pepper, extra virgin olive oil, grated pecorino cheese.

Preparation:

1. Finely chop basil, garlic, and capers. Place in a bowl, cover with extra virgin olive oil and set aside to marinate for at least 5 hours.
2. Bring a large pot of salted water to a boil and cook the pasta until al dente. Drain well and let it cool before transferring to a salad or mixing bowl.
3. Slice the cherry tomatoes in half and add them to the pasta. Dice the fresh mozzarella into 2 cm cubes and add to the pasta.
4. Add the marinated mixture of basil, garlic, and capers, along with olives, chili pepper, and grated pecorino cheese to the pasta.
5. Toss well and adjust with more olive oil or pecorino if desired.

Notes:

_____

_____

_____

_____

_____

Places & Traditions

Venus Temple (Erice)

The Temple of Venus rose on Erice's fortress. Erice, the son of Venus and Bute, built the temple on the rock to thank his mother for saving his father from the Sirens. This is why Aphrodite became the protector of sailors.

Sailors, whether friends or foes, from east to west, visited the fortress daily seeking protection and love from the goddess and her priestesses.

In ancient times, on the 15th of August every year, men, women, and the priestesses of the goddess celebrated the doves' flight, symbolizing Venus' journey to the Sanctuary of Cyprus and her return to Sicily nine days later.

Erice, born from the union of Venus and the Argonaut Bute, was the King of the Elimi in Sicily, and he founded the city of Erice on the mountain that now bears his name. He erected a magnificent temple in honour of Ericina (Aphrodite).

Erice met his demise at the hands of Hercules for stealing an ox from Geryon.

View from the Castle – Erice, Trapani

Pasta 'cche Sarde 'a Palermitana

(Pasta with sardines and wild fennel)

A typical dish of the west coast of the island.

Ingredients (serves 4):

400 g bucatini, 400 g of fresh sardines boned, 2 bunches of wild fennel, 1 onion, 4 salted anchovy fillets, 1 tbsp tomato puree, 1 tbsp pine nuts, 1 tbsp raisins, saffron, toasted breadcrumbs, extra virgin olive oil, salt and pepper.

Preparation:

1. Clean the wild fennel and boil it in a large pan of salted water.
2. Drain the fennel and keep the cooking water, then chop coarsely and set aside.
3. Separately, chop the onion and fry until golden, then add the anchovies and the tomato puree, stirring with a wooden spoon until the fillets dissolve.
4. Add the sardines, the wild fennel, raisins, pine nuts, and saffron. Season to taste with salt and pepper and cook for a few minutes, adding a ladleful of the fennel water.
5. Bring the remaining water to boil again and cook the pasta al dente.
6. Drain and mix with half the sauce. Place the pasta in the dishes and pour the remaining sauce and sprinkle with the toasted breadcrumbs. Serve hot.

Notes:

_____

_____

_____

_____

_____

_____

Pasta alla Norma

(Pasta with eggplants)

This Catania dish typically features Ricotta Salata cheese. The semi-hard, salted ricotta imparts a distinct flavour, and it is usually available in specialty shops. If necessary, you can substitute it with pecorino cheese, resulting in a slightly different but still delicious taste. The dish is named "Alla Norma" in honour of the composer Vincenzo Bellini, who was born in Catania and composed the Opera "Norma."

Ingredients (serves 4):

400 g maccheroni or fusilli, 10 ripe tomatoes or tinned peeled tomatoes, 1 garlic clove, 1 aubergine, 1 tsp sugar, 100 g grated ricotta salata, extra virgin olive oil, salt, pepper, basil

Preparation:

1. Slice the eggplants, sprinkle them with salt, and let them rest for half an hour in a colander to remove the bitter liquid.
2. Prepare the tomato sauce by chopping the tomatoes in a pan over low heat. Add a pinch of salt and cook for about ten minutes, then add garlic, pepper, a tsp. of sugar, and oil. Simmer until the sauce thickens.
3. Wash and dry the eggplants, then fry them in abundant hot oil, chop coarsely, and set aside.
4. Cook the pasta al dente in salted water, drain well, and add half the tomato sauce.
5. Pour onto serving dishes, and cover with the remaining sauce and the chopped eggplants.

6. Finish the dish by sprinkling with ricotta salata and basil leaves. Serve hot.

Notes:

_____

_____

_____

_____

_____

Cannelloni 'cco sucu

(Cannelloni with meat sauce)

Ingredients (serves 4):

For the pasta: 300 g flour, 2 eggs.

For the stuffing: 300 g of minced beef or pork, cooked with tomato sauce, 200 g peas, cooked with spring onion, 80 g grated caciocavallo or parmesan cheese, 200 g tuma cheese, pepper.

Preparation:

1. Make a dough with the flour and eggs. Roll out until very thin and cut into 10 cm squares.
2. Finely chop the cooked meat and mix it with the peas and onions, the tuma cheese (this could be replaced with a soft cheese like provola), half of the caciocavallo (or parmesan), ground pepper, and a few tablespoons of the meat sauce.
3. Cook the lasagne in boiling water a few at a time, strain, and lay separately on a clean cloth.
4. Spoon a strip of the filling onto each lasagne, roll the lasagne up, and place side by side in a greased oven dish.
5. Cover with meat sauce and sprinkle with the remaining caciocavallo (or parmesan).
6. Bake in a hot oven for about 20 minutes or until the top is golden brown and serve hot.

Notes:

_____

_____

_____

_____

_____

_____

Pasta Rustica

(Pasta with broccoli and olives)

Ingredients (Serves 4):

350 g pasta (penne or fusilli), 400 g broccoli, 1 garlic clove, 2 anchovy fillets, 8 black olives, 2 tbsp red wine, chili pepper, 1 tsp tomato puree, 8 tbsp olive oil, salt and pepper.

Preparation:

1. Remove any tough stalks and leaves from the broccoli and boil in a large saucepan of salted water for ten minutes. Strain but save the water.
2. Lightly fry the broccoli with half the oil, the clove of garlic lightly crushed, and pepper, then add the wine and simmer, breaking the broccoli up into small pieces with a wooden spoon.
3. In another pan, lightly fry the anchovy fillets in the rest of the oil with the pitted olives and a pinch of chili pepper.
4. Add the tomato puree and mix for a few seconds, then add this mixture to the broccoli along with a ladleful of the water the broccoli was cooked in. Simmer for 3-4 minutes then turn it off and remove the garlic clove.
5. In the meantime, bring the broccoli water back to a boil and boil the pasta in it.
6. Strain the pasta leaving a small amount of water in the bottom of the pan, add the sauce and pour onto a serving dish. Serve immediately.

Notes:

_____

_____

_____

_____

_____

_____

Puppetti ri risu

(Rice rissoles)

Ingredients (serves 4):

500 g rice, 50 g grated cheese, 50 g breadcrumb, 1 garlic clove, parsley, salt, black pepper, 3 eggs, extra virgin olive oil.

Preparation:

1. Cook the rice and drain it well.
2. Leave it to cool and mix it with the breadcrumb, cheese, salt, black pepper, chopped parsley, and garlic.
3. Optionally, you can add chopped smoked ham or sausages.
4. Mix the compound with whisked eggs and give the rissoles an oval shape.
5. Fry them in generous hot oil.

Notes:

_____

_____

_____

_____

_____

_____

Scala dei Turchi – Trapani

Pasta 'cca sassa a' carrittera

(Pasta with Tomato sauce "carrettiera" style)

Ingredients (serves 4):

400 g spaghetti or fusilli, 600 g ripe tomatoes, 1 garlic clove, 1 bunch of basil, salt, extra virgin olive oil.

Preparation:

1. Wash the tomatoes, peel them, and finely chop them.
2. Place them in a pan with the crushed garlic. After a few minutes, add the basil.
3. Let the excess water evaporate and add salt and olive oil. A teaspoon of sugar is required if the sauce is sharp.
4. Cook the pasta al dente, drain it well, and dress with the hot sauce. Serve with a bit of grated cheese on top.

Notes:

_____

_____

_____

_____

_____

_____

Cavateddi 'cco sucu fintu

(Cavatelli Pasta with fake meat sauce)

The traditional pasta with meat sauce would include the presence of meat, either minced or in pieces. As we mentioned, not being able to afford the more expensive products, people replaced them with more affordable ones or, as in this case, eliminated them altogether. Hence the name "Sugo Finto" (Fake Sauce) since meat is not part of the ingredients.

Ingredients (serves 4):

400 g cavatelli pasta, 1 onion, 1 tbsp double-concentrated tomato, 300 g peeled potato, 1 tsp wild fennel seeds (or aniseed).

Preparation:

1. Fry the chopped onion and add the concentrated tomato. Add a bit of water and stir well.
2. Add the fennel seeds and a glass of water and let the compound simmer on low heat for 15/20 min.
3. Add the potatoes cut into quarters and cook until they are ready.
4. Cook the cavatelli al dente, drain well, and dress with the hot sauce. Serve with a bit of grated cheese on top.

Notes:

_____

_____

_____

_____

_____

_____

Ragusa Ibla – San Giorgio Cathedral

Places & Traditions

U Carrettu - Sicilian Horse Carts

The art of cart creation is almost a lost one, kept alive by the diligence and dedication of just a few talented craftsmen—simultaneously carpenters, ironsmiths, and artists. In the paintings on the carts, Sicilian kings and knights stride alongside legends like Roland—called Orlando in Italian. Normans fight Moors, and Sicilians combat Angevins.

In centuries past, these works of art were ubiquitous in Sicily. The few that remain, and the few that are created each year, seem to represent more than another era.

They symbolize a way of life and the fact that Sicily's unique medieval history has never been far from the popular mind. A few antique carts can be seen, and new ones purchased, in the Sicilian Cart Museum behind the apse of Palermo Cathedral.

Couscous 'A Trapanisa

(Couscous Trapani Style)

The proximity of Trapani and Tunis, along with the commercial and social exchanges that intertwined the two cities over the centuries, allowed a fusion of cultural topics from architecture to food. Trapani absorbed Tunisian couscous culture, adding its own Sicilian touch to this typical Arab dish. Sicilian Couscous alla Trapanese is a main course, and its unusual feature is the combination of fish and chicken in the same dish.

Ingredients for the sauce:

1 large chopped red onion, ½ glass extra virgin olive oil, 700 g blanched and seeded tomatoes cut into large pieces, about 2 pounds fish heads and tails wrapped in gauze, black pepper, hot red pepper flakes, a bunch of parsley, 6 large garlic cloves peeled, basil leaves left whole, 4 tbsp tomato paste, 700 ml chicken broth.

Ingredients for the fish and chicken:

6 medium-sized calamari, cleaned and cut into 1 cm rings, 1 kg of different types of non-oily fish, cut into large pieces with bones (langoustine, the small lobsters, are optional), 1 large lemon, coarse-grained salt, 1 chicken (about 1 ½ kg), cut into 10 pieces with all the extra fat removed.

Ingredients for precooked couscous:

Follow the procedure printed on the box, adding oil (not butter), as well as the bay leaves and ground saffron.

Ingredients for the broth:

3 litres of very light chicken broth, 4 bay leaves, a large pinch of ground saffron, 4 medium-sized carrots, scraped and cut into large pieces.

Ingredients to serve:

3 or 4 scampi for decoration, 15 sprigs parsley, leaves only, coarsely chopped.

Preparation:

1. Soak the calamari and fish pieces in a large bowl of cold water with the lemon, cut in half and squeezed, and a little coarse salt for a half-hour.
2. Place the 3 litres of broth along with the bay leaves, saffron, and carrots in a stockpot and bring it to a boil over medium heat.
3. Line a colander with a thick piece of gauze, then mix the prepared couscous with the bay leaves and put it in the prepared colander.
4. Fold the gauze over the top and insert the colander into the stockpot containing the boiling broth. Let it simmer for 1 hour. (Tightly cover the colander with a lid or aluminium foil. It is important that the stockpot and the colander are the same size, but if there is a lot of space between the stockpot and the colander, you can make a dough with flour and water and attach it all around the opening to keep the steam from escaping.)
5. Meanwhile, heat the oil in a large pan over medium heat. When the oil is warm, add the onions to the pan; sauté for 5 minutes, stirring constantly.
6. Add the tomatoes and cook for 15 minutes, stirring every so often with a wooden spoon.
7. Then, add the fish heads and tails with their gauze wrapping and cook for an additional 15 minutes, turning the "bags" over 2 or 3 times.
8. Season with salt, pepper, and the hot pepper flakes.

9. Finely chop parsley and garlic together on a board. Add the chopped ingredients, along with the whole basil leaves, to the pan. Mix thoroughly and cook for an additional 5 minutes.

10. Dissolve the tomato paste in the broth and pour it into the pan. Reduce the heat and simmer for 1 hour, allowing the liquid to reduce by half.

11. Remove and discard the gauze along with all its fish bones.

12. Taste the sauce to check for seasoning.

13. Begin by adding the fish that require at least 35 minutes of cooking time, such as calamari, to the broth. Introduce the remaining fish and chicken pieces, adjusting the timing as needed. The chicken should be fully cooked within 20 minutes.

14. Open the gauze in the colander, thoroughly mix the couscous to ensure no lumps have formed, and close it again. Let it cook for an additional hour.

15. Once the sauce is ready and the fish and chicken are fully cooked, transfer the couscous to a large serving platter. Pour the entire sauce over the couscous, arrange all the fish and chicken (with or without scampi) on top, and sprinkle with parsley. Serve hot.

Piazza Armerina – Villa del Casale Mosaics – Bikini

Pani cottu 'cca sassa

(Cooked bread with tomato sauce)

This recipe was used by poor people in order to eat the homemade bread to the last crumb, even days after the bread was baked.

Ingredients (serves 4):

½ kg stale bread, tomato sauce, pecorino cheese as needed, extra virgin olive oil, salt, black pepper.

Preparation:

1. Cut the bread into big pieces and put in boiling salted water for about 5 min.
2. Drain well and dress with the tomato sauce, grated pecorino cheese and black pepper.
3. It is also possible to add dried tomato or anchovies as an option.

Notes:

_____

_____

_____

_____

_____

Pasta 'cca cucuzza

(Pasta with zucchini)

Ingredients (serves 4):

200 gr. short pasta, 1 medium onion, 1 long white zucchini, 2 fresh ripe tomatoes, olive oil, salt.

Preparation:

1. Fry the chopped onion in a pan and add the peeled and chopped tomato, then add the chopped zucchini.
2. Stir well and add hot water until the mixture is completely covered.
3. When the zucchini are nearly cooked, add more water, correct the salt, and add the pasta.
4. Serve hot, adding grated cheese and pepper to taste.

Stomboli eruption, Aeolian Islands

Pasta 'cca muddica

(Pasta with anchovies and breadcrumbs)

Breadcrumbs were often used, toasted, in Sicily as a substitute for grated cheese by those who could not afford even this basic ingredient: some used to call toasted breadcrumbs the 'poor man's Caciocavallo.

Ingredients (serves 4):

400 g pasta, 8 salted anchovies, boned, 1 tbsp tomato puree, 2 tbsp capers, 120 g toasted breadcrumbs, 1 garlic clove, chopped parsley, olive oil, salt, pepper.

Preparation:

1. Toast the breadcrumbs (preferably in an iron skillet), stirring continuously. Before they turn brown, add a little oil and mix until the oil starts to sizzle, and the breadcrumbs turn a nice golden colour.
2. Separately heat some oil in a frying pan with the garlic, remove from heat, and add the anchovies, mashing with a fork until they achieve a creamy consistency.
3. Add the tomato puree and capers and stir over moderate heat for a few minutes. Remove from heat and add the chopped parsley and a pinch of pepper.
4. Boil the pasta in a large pan of salted water, drain, and cover with the anchovies' sauce. Sprinkle with the toasted breadcrumbs and serve immediately.

Notes:

_____

_____

_____

_____

_____

Pasta 'cco niuru ri siccia

(Pasta with black ink sauce)

Ingredients (serves 4):

400 g spaghetti, 300 g fresh cuttlefish with their black ink bags, 1 onion, 1 bunch of parsley, 1 tbsp tomato puree, extra virgin olive oil, salt, black pepper, ½ glass white wine.

Preparation:

1. Remove the backbone of the cuttlefish. Carefully remove the ink bag and keep it separated. Wash the cuttlefish and cut it into strips.
2. Brown the finely chopped onion in a pan and add the chopped parsley. Add the tomato puree and the cuttlefish strips. Let the sauce cook on low heat, and after a while, add the ink.
3. Stir well and add the half glass of white wine. Add a bit of water and let it cook for half an hour.
4. Cook the pasta "al dente," drain well, pour it into a serving dish, and add the black sauce. As an option, it is possible to add some grated, salted ricotta cheese.

Notes:

_____

_____

_____

_____

_____

_____

_____

Spaghetti 'cche vonguli

(Spaghetti with clams)

Ingredients (serves 4):

400 g spaghetti, 1 kg clams, 4 garlic cloves, ½ glass white wine, 1 bunch fresh parsley, extra virgin olive oil, salt, chilli pepper.

Preparation:

1. Bring a large pot of salted water to boil and add the spaghetti. Cook over high heat, stirring the pasta from time to time to prevent sticking, according to package instructions.
2. In a large, deep pan, brown the garlic in the olive oil over medium heat until lightly translucent. Then, add the clams, white wine, and chilli pepper.
3. Cover the pan and simmer over low heat, stirring occasionally. Once all the clams open and release their juices, immediately remove from heat and salt to taste.
4. When the spaghetti are al dente, strain and place them in a large bowl. Pour the clams and juices over the pasta, add the chopped parsley, and, if desired, ground black pepper. Serve immediately.

Notes:

_____

_____

_____

_____

_____

_____

Pasta agghia, ogghiu e pipiolu

(Pasta with garlic, oil and red chilli pepper)

This dish is very easy and popular. Particularly during the summer, it is prepared with friends around midnight and is called "spaghettata di mezzanotte" (midnight nosh-up of spaghetti).

Ingredients (serves 4):

400 g spaghetti, 2 garlic cloves, 1 bunch of parsley, red hot chili pepper, extra virgin olive oil, salt.

Preparation:

1. Cook the spaghetti "al dente". Drain well and reserve two tablespoons of the cooking water.
2. In a frying pan over low heat, sauté the garlic in the olive oil until golden. Add the chilies and the reserved cooking water.
3. Add the spaghetti and season with the chopped parsley, salt, and pepper.
4. Toss so that the spaghetti is coated in the olive oil mixture, ensuring everything is well combined.

Notes:

_____

_____

_____

_____

_____

_____

Ravioli 'cca ricotta

(Ravioli with ricotta)

Ingredients (serves 4):

For the pasta:

500 g hard wheat flour, 2 eggs, 3 tbsp olive oil, salt.

For the filling:

500 g ricotta, 2 yolks, 3 tbsp grated cheese, black pepper.

Preparation:

1. Mix the flour with the ingredients and add a bit of water if required. The consistency of the dough must be quite hard.
2. Roll out a thin layer with a rolling pin or, even better, with a machine for making pasta.
3. In a bowl mix ricotta with the other ingredients using a fork.
4. Place a layer of seasoned and well-mixed ricotta on the pasta. It is my habit to add a little bit of nutmeg to the ricotta compound for a nice aroma.
5. Put another layer of pasta on top and cut the ravioli shape with a pastry wheel.
6. Place the cut ravioli on a floured tray.
7. Cook the ravioli in salted abundant water until they float.
8. Drain them well and dress with pork sauce (sugo di maiale) and some grated cheese.

Notes:

_____

_____

_____

_____

_____

_____

Spaghetti 'all'eoliana

(Spaghetti Aeolian style)

Ingredients (serves 4):

400 g spaghetti, 12 ripe cherry tomatoes, 4 garlic cloves, 60 g pitted green olives, 60 g pitted black olives, 2 tbsp capers, oregano, basil leaves, extra virgin olive oil, salt, chilli pepper.

Preparation:

1. Slice the tomatoes in half, chop the garlic, and coarsely mince the olives. Rinse the capers and tear the basil leaves.
2. Bring a large pot of salted water to a boil and add the spaghetti, cooking over high heat. Cook the spaghetti according to package instructions, stirring the pasta from time to time to prevent sticking.
3. In the meantime, lightly brown the garlic in the olive oil in a large pan over moderate heat, cooking for a few moments before adding the chopped tomatoes, minced olives, and capers.
4. When the tomatoes are at a half-cooking point, add the oregano, basil, and crushed chili pepper. Salt to taste. If the sauce becomes too dry, add a spoonful or two of pasta water to loosen the sauce. Remove from the hob and set aside.
5. When the pasta is al dente, drain and simmer with the sauce until evenly combined. Serve immediately.

Notes:

_____

_____

_____

_____

_____

Pasta 'o furnu

(Baked pasta)

"Anelletti" is a typical shape of pasta that is characteristic of Sicilian tradition. Many other shapes of pasta are actually used on the island with many different fillings. Baked anelletti in particular are traditional in Palermo where the dish is prepared during public festivities. Below is the recipe for the Palermo-style baked pasta.

Ingredients (serves 6):

500 g anelletti, 200 g grated caciocavallo or pecorino cheese, 200g minced veal, 100 g fresh pecorino, 100 g minced pork, 2 tbsp tomato puree, 1 onion, 100 g breadcrumbs, 1 glass red wine, olive oil, salt, pepper.

Preparation:

1. Brown in a pan the finely chopped onion, add the minced veal and pork, raise the heat and add the red wine. Let it fry for a couple of minutes and then add the tomato puree and 500 ml hot water.
2. Reduce the heat to a minimum, correct the salt, add a pinch of black pepper and let it simmering for 30 minutes.
3. Cook the anelletti in salted water. When anelletti are "al dente", switch the heat off and drain them well. Mix the anelletti with the sauce, add the grated caciocavallo, and the fresh pecorino in slices.
4. Add the pasta in an oily baking tin sprinkled with breadcrumbs.
5. Sprinkle the top with a generous amount of breadcrumbs, some olive oil and put in the oven at 180° C for 20 minutes.

Notes:

_____

_____

_____

_____

_____

_____

Risotto alla Pescatora

(Seafood Risotto)

This delicious risotto is fabulous if you can get fresh ingredients. This is an excellent recipe during summertime.

Ingredients (serves 4):

400 g Arborio rice, 500 g clams, 300 g mussels, 200 g little squid, 200 g prawns, 1 big ripe tomato, ½ glass white wine, fish (non-oily) for broth, 1 onion, 2 garlic cloves, 1 stalk of celery, parsley, salt, pepper, chili pepper.

Preparation:

1. Put the water in a pan, add 1/2 the onion, carrot, celery, salt and pepper, and the fish, and let it simmer for at least 20 minutes.
2. Put the clams and mussels into another pan, add 2 glasses of water, and put on the heat for about 8 minutes, till the shells open. Don't discard the cooking water but filter it as you'll use it later.
3. Clean the prawns and squids. Finely chop the onion, and the tomato, crush the garlic, brown it in olive oil and then add the squid cut into pieces and the prawns and cook for another 3 minutes.
4. Add some salt and chilli pepper if you like.
5. Add the rice, mix well and cook for a couple of minutes before adding the wine. When the wine has evaporated, start adding one or two ladles of broth at a time and stir constantly for about 20 minutes.
6. Add the clams and mussels and keep adding stock and stirring. Cook until the risotto thickens, and the rice is soft.
7. At the very end add a tablespoon of butter for a creamy consistency.
8. Serve immediately with chopped parsley on top.

Notes:

_____

_____

_____

_____

_____

_____

Myths and Legends

U' Liotru (The elephant of Catania)

U Liotru, or the "Fontana dell'Elefante", is the symbol of Catania. Assembled in 1736 by Giovanni Battista Vaccarini, it portrays an ancient lavic stone elephant and is topped by an Egyptian obelisk from Syene.

The Sicilian name u Liotru is a phonetic change of Heliodorus, a nobleman who lived in Catania in VIII century A.D. After trying without success to become bishop of the city, he became a sorcerer. The myth claims that the statue itself was created by the Catania magician, who sculpted it using the lava from Mount Etna and brought it to life with a magical breath. It is said that Heliodorus used Liotru to move around the city and all the way to Constantinople, playing pranks on the citizens of Catania along the way, and disturbing the religious services in the city. After 13 years, Leone II, who had become Bishop instead of Heliodorus, tired of his provocations condemned him to the stake.

The mystery surrounds the legendary magician Heliodorus' fate: according to the legend, he caught fire and vanished into his own ashes, leaving behind the Liotru, crafted by himself, to the people of Catania who have made it their symbol.

The presence of an elephant in the millenary history of Catania is surely connected to both zoo-archaeology and popular creeds. In fact, the prehistoric fauna of Sicily from the Upper Palaeolithic included dwarf elephants. Palaeontologist Othenio Abel suggested that the presence of dwarf elephants in Sicily may be the origin of the legend of the Cyclops.

Ancient Greeks, after finding the skulls of dwarf elephants, about twice the size of a human skull, with a large central nasal cavity (mistaken for a large single eye socket) supposed that they were skulls of giants with a single eye.

The Museum of Mineralogy, Palaeontology, and Volcanology in Catania holds the integral unburied skeleton of an "Elephas Falconeri" in an excellent state of conservation.

Catania – Piazza Duomo and "U' Liotru"

Spaghetti 'cche cozzi

(Spaghetti with mussels)

Ingredients (serves 4):

400 g spaghetti, 1 kg mussels, 4 garlic cloves, ½ glass white wine, 1 bunch fresh parsley, extra virgin olive oil, salt, chili pepper.

Preparation:

1. Bring a large pot of salted water to a boil, add the spaghetti and cook over high heat.
2. Cook spaghetti according to package instructions stirring the pasta from time to time to prevent sticking.
3. In a large, deep pan, brown the garlic in the olive oil over medium heat and cook until lightly translucent.
4. Add the mussels, the white wine, and add the chili pepper. Cover the pan and simmer over low heat, stirring occasionally.
5. Once all the mussels open and release their juices, immediately remove from heat and salt to taste.
6. When the spaghetti is al dente, strain and place in a large bowl.
7. Pour the mussels and juices over the pasta, add the chopped parsley, and if desired, ground black pepper. Serve immediately.

Notes:

_____

_____

_____

_____

_____

_____

Pasta 'cco maccu

(Pasta with broad beans cream)

Maccu is a Sicilian dish made from a cream obtained by cooking dried broad beans. It is a delicious and traditional preparation.

Ingredients (serves 4):

800 g dry broad beans, extra virgin olive oil, salt.

Preparation:

1. Soak the broad beans in lightly salted water overnight.
2. Place the broad beans in a saucepan, cover with water, and cook over low heat. Stir frequently until you obtain a smooth puree.
3. Add olive oil and adjust the salt to taste.
4. Maccu is now ready to be served hot, alone or with some chunks of toasted bread.
5. If you want to serve maccu with pasta, add the pasta just before the final cooking point to create a delicious winter pasta soup known as "pasta 'cco maccu re favi."

Notes:

_____

_____

_____

_____

_____

_____

Places & Traditions

Opera dei Pupi

"Pupi" became popular in Sicily late in the Middle Ages, during the fifteenth century, and marionettes are still considered an important part of Sicilian folk culture.

Sicilian puppet theatre (opera dei pupi) or, more properly, "marionette theatre," developed into its present form in the eighteenth century. (Strictly speaking, "puppets" fit over the hand, while marionettes are figures controlled by strings, but in common parlance, the terms are often used interchangeably; what we're describing are actually marionettes.)

Typically, the marionettes and their theatre depict medieval characters and legendary events loosely based on history. There's Orlando (Roland), one of Charlemagne's knights, and the Norman knights of King Roger of Sicily, and Saracens (Moors): baroque paladins, actually, because their costumes often resemble sixteenth-century decoration more than medieval armour and clothes.

The marionettes themselves are made of wood with cloth and metal accoutrements. A handful of marionette makers still work in Sicily, particularly in Palermo, Catania, and Messina, and sell many of their creations as souvenirs.

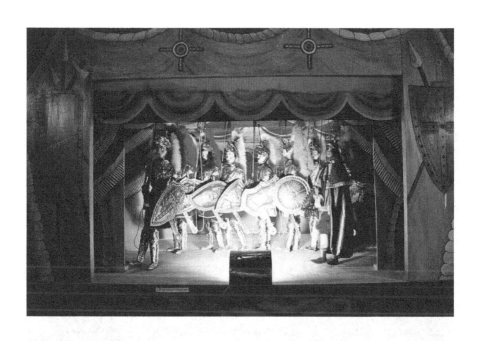

Puppet Theater by Mimmo Cuticchio, Via Bara all'Olivella – Palermo

Fichi d'India (Opuntia ficus-indica), Cefalù –Palermo

Le 'Mpanate

(or "Scacciate" or "Scacciuna")

This dish is typical of the area around Siracusa and Ragusa on the east coast of Sicily, where I come from. These delicacies are typically made during Easter or Christmas and were imported by the Spanish, who learned these recipes from the Arabs themselves, but they can be prepared and enjoyed all year round.

Prepare the dough for 'mpanate.

Ingredients:

500 g hard wheat flour, 1 tsp salt, 25 g brewer's yeast, 1 glass warm water, 2 tbsp olive oil. Pour the flour giving it a basin shape.

Preparation:

1. Dissolve the yeast in a bit of warm water and pour it in the middle of the flour and then add the remaining water with the salt and start kneading.
2. Work well and for a long period of time the dough, and add the oil a bit per time. Cover the dough with flour and cover with a clean tablecloth. Let it rise in a lukewarm place for at least 30 min.
3. Cut the risen dough into two portions and make two discs with a rolling pin. Place one of them in an oily baking tin, stuff with the prepared filling and cover with the other disc, joining firmly the edges with the fingertips making a twine. Prick the surface with a fork several times, and put in a hot oven at 250° for about 30 min. depending on the filling.

Notes:

_____

_____

_____

_____

_____

_____

'Mpanata ri brocculi or cauluciuri

(Broccoli or cauliflower filling)

Ingredients (serves 4):

1 kg of broccoli or cauliflower, 500 g sausage, 1 garlic clove, salt, black pepper, chilli pepper, extra virgin olive oil.

Use the dough prepared according to the recipe on previous page "Le 'Mpanate":

Preparation:

1. Wash the broccoli, cut in pieces and put in boiling salted water.
2. Drain it well before it is fully cooked and let it cool down and add the finely chopped garlic, pepper, the chilli and the raw sausage cut in pieces.
3. Mix well and put in the baking tin with the first disc of dough. It is possible to add some grated cheese or mozzarella in pieces. Dress with olive oil and cover with the other disk of dough.
4. Prick the surface with a fork several times, and put in a hot oven at 250° for about 30 min.

Notes:

_____

_____

_____

_____

_____

_____

'Mpanata ri patate e cipudda

('Mpanata with potatoes and onions)

Ingredients (serves 4)

800 g peeled potatoes, 500 g white onions, salt, pepper, extra virgin olive oil.

Use the dough prepared according to the recipe on previous page "Le 'Mpanate":

Preparation:

1. Cut the potatoes into tiny slices, add the sliced onions and dress with salt, black pepper and olive oil.
2. Put the mixture in a baking tin with the first disc of dough. Additionally, it is possible to add some grated cheese or ricotta cheese in pieces.
3. Dress with olive oil and cover with the other disk of dough.
4. Prick the surface with a fork several times, and place in a hot oven at 250° for about 30 min.

Notes:

_____

_____

_____

_____

_____

_____

149

'Mpanata ri spinaci

('Mpanata with spinaches)

Ingredients (serves 4)

2 kg spinach, 350 g sausage, 1 garlic clove, extra virgin olive oil, salt, pepper.

Use the dough prepared according to the recipe on previous page "Le 'Mpanate".

Preparation:

1. Wash and cook the spinach in lightly salted water. Drain it well and let it cool.
2. Cut and dress with garlic, salt and black pepper and place on the bottom of the dough in a baking tin. Brown the sausage, cut it in small pieces and add it to the spinach.
3. Add some dried tomatoes if you would like, dress with olive oil and cover with the other disk of dough.
4. Prick the surface with a fork several times, brush it with olive oil, and put it in a hot oven at 250° for about 30 min.

Notes:

_____

_____

_____

_____

_____

_____

Aeolian Islands – Sunset

Meat

Agneddu a spizzatinu

(Stew of lamb)

Ingredients (serves 4):

1 kg lamb, 1 garlic clove, 2 ripe tomatoes, ½ kg potatoes, salt, extra virgin olive oil, black pepper, 1 bunch parsley.

Instructions:

1. Lightly boil the lamb with some lemon.
2. In a skillet, fry the garlic first. Then, add the chopped parsley and the tomatoes cut into small pieces.
3. Add the lamb to the skillet and pour in half a glass of red wine. Let it evaporate.
4. Fry for a few minutes, and then add water until it covers the meat.
5. After 15 minutes, add the potatoes in pieces and cook for another 20 minutes on low heat. Optionally, you can use the broth to dress pasta.

Notes:

_____

_____

_____

_____

_____

_____

Agneddu 'nfurnatu

(Baked lamb)

Ingredients (serves 4):

1.5 kg lamb, 2 ripe tomatoes, 1 garlic clove, 1 small white onion, 1 bunch of parsley, 800 g potatoes, extra virgin olive oil, salt, black pepper.

Preparation:

1. Put the lamb pieces in an oily baking tin.
2. Dress the meat with the tomatoes in pieces, chopped onion, chopped garlic, parsley, salt, and black pepper.
3. Cover the tin with foil and put it in the hot oven.
4. At the half-cooking point, add the potatoes in big pieces and pour in half a glass of red wine. Cover again.
5. Ten minutes before reaching the cooking point, remove the foil to allow a crispy layer to form.

Notes:

_____

_____

_____

_____

_____

_____

Vavaluci, Crastuna, 'Ntuppateddi

(Snails)

This is a dish I am particularly fond of. When I was a child, my father used to take me out to catch snails after the rain. It was truly delightful, especially when we went out during the night. I still remember the excitement of walking in the countryside with an oil lantern or a torch and a wicker basket, searching for snails.

There are different kinds of snails, and Sicilian people have various names for them. I come from the southeast coast, where we call the small white or striped ones "vavaluci" or "babbaini" and the large ones "crastuna." There are also others with a brown shell and a grey body called "ntuppateddi" because they seal the shell with a thick white material. In Sicilian, the act of sealing is translated as "ntuppare," from which the name "ntuppateddi" originates.

Snail meat is a truly healthy food, containing 13% proteins and only 1.7% fat. The particular chemical properties of the fat promote the removal of human cholesterol through the biliary ducts.

Notes:

_____

_____

_____

_____

_____

_____

Vavaluci 'ccull'agghia e l'ogghiu

(Snails with garlic and oil)

Ingredients (serves 4):

1 kg snails, garlic, olive oil, parsley, vinegar, salt, pepper, raw pasta

Preparation:

1. Place the snails in a wicker basket with some raw pasta at the bottom. Allow them to clear for a week, then wash them by rubbing them under running water.
2. Transfer them to a saucepan, cover them with water, and cook on very low heat for about 15 minutes from when the water starts boiling.
3. Meanwhile, in a pan, brown two cloves of crushed garlic in olive oil. Add the drained snails to the pan, season with salt and abundant pepper. Let them simmer for a few minutes on low heat, mixing well.
4. Add finely chopped parsley and a splash of vinegar. Allow it to evaporate, remove from heat, and serve hot.

Notes:

_____

_____

_____

_____

_____

_____

Crastuna 'cco pummaroru

(Snails with tomato sauce)

Ingredients (serves 4):

1 kg brown snails (crastuna), 700 g ripe tomatoes, 1 onion, extra virgin olive oil, salt, pepper, raw pasta.

Preparation:

1. Place the crastuna in a wicker basket with some raw pasta at the bottom. Allow them to clear for a week, then wash them by rubbing them under running water.
2. Transfer them to a saucepan, cover with water, and cook on very low heat for about 15 minutes from when the water starts boiling.
3. In the meantime, in a pan, brown a big, sliced onion in olive oil and add the chopped tomatoes. Adjust the salt and pepper and let it simmer for about 20 minutes.
4. Drain the crastuna and add them to the sauce, cooking together for another 5 minutes while mixing well.

Notes:

_____

_____

_____

_____

_____

_____

Carni 'cco sucu e patati

(Meat with tomato sauce and potatoes)

Ingredients (serves 4):

500 g pork meat, 2 potatoes, onion, carrots, celery, concentrated tomato, salt, black pepper.

Preparation:

1. In a saucepan with half a glass of olive oil, add onion, carrot, and a stalk of chopped celery, and lightly fry them.
2. Add the meat in pieces and fry on low heat. Season with salt and pepper and add half a glass of red wine and a spoonful of concentrated tomato.
3. Cover and let it cook on low heat. After half an hour, add the potatoes in big pieces. Let the meat cook for another 20 minutes and serve hot.
4. The meat and potatoes can also be a main course when served with chunks of toasted bread on the side.
5. The sauce is a fabulous dressing for tagliatelle or maccheroni.

Notes:

_____

_____

_____

_____

_____

_____

Cunigghiu a' stimpirata

(Rabbit with vinegar and mint)

This dish is not difficult, but it will take a bit of time to prepare. It is worth doing it, however, as it is delicious. In the past, wild rabbits were used, whose meat has an intense flavour. Hence the addition of aromas such as mint and the addition of vinegar to moderate the strong taste.

Ingredients (serves 4):

1 rabbit, approximately 1 ½ kg, potatoes, carrots, olives (both green and black), onion, celery, basil, parsley, garlic, dry tomatoes, mint, capers, salt, extra virgin olive oil, white vinegar.

Preparation:

1. Put the cut rabbit in a non-sticking pan without oil and let it brown on very low heat, allowing the liquid to drain from the meat.
2. When there is no more water, add olive oil and salt and let it brown for a few more minutes. Add a glass of white wine and maintain on the hob until fully cooked.
3. Fry the potatoes and pull them apart, taking care to dry them of the oil.
4. In a saucepan, put half a glass of extra virgin olive oil, chopped onion, celery, carrots, and garlic, and fry everything. At the halfway point, add olives, capers, mint (important ingredient), basil, and chopped dry tomato.
5. Add the rabbit and keep it on the heat, adding a bit of olive oil. Add the potatoes and another bit of mint.
6. Add half a glass of vinegar at the end, cover the saucepan, switch off the heat, and let it cool down.

166

7. It is possible to serve the dish hot or cold.

Notes:

_____

_____

_____

_____

_____

_____

Myths and Legends

Cocalus (Ragusa)

Cocalus was the king of Kamikos in Sicily. After the escape of Daedalus and Icarus from King Minos' imprisonment, and the subsequent death of Icarus, Daedalus arrived in Sicily, where he was welcomed by King Cocalus. Minos, however, was determined to find Daedalus and sent word to all the kings of the known world, stating that whoever could solve a particular puzzle would be richly rewarded. Minos believed that only Daedalus could solve the difficult task: of threading a thread through a spiral seashell. Cocalus, aware that Daedalus could solve the puzzle, showed it to him. Daedalus pierced a hole in the tip of the conch shell, smeared it with honey, and tied the thread around an ant. Attracted by the honey, the ant wound its way through the spirals of the empty shell, taking the thread with it. Cocalus joyfully announced to Minos that the puzzle had been solved, never suspecting that he was thus betraying Daedalus, the most-wanted fugitive in Minoan Crete. So, Minos travelled to Sicily and demanded Daedalus be handed over to him. Cocalus desired a good relationship with the Minoans. However, skilled architects and craftsmen were hard to find. So, instead of immediately handing the craftsman over to Minos, he convinced him to take a bath to purify himself after the long journey, and there, with the help of his daughter, he killed him.

King Cocalus

Frittata 'cche sparici

(Asparagus frittata)

Ingredients (serves 4):

6 large eggs, 500 g fresh asparagus, chopped parsley, extra virgin olive oil, 2 tbsp freshly grated parmesan or pecorino cheese, 2 tbsp breadcrumbs, salt.

Preparation:

1. Wash the asparagus and break off the tender parts. Put the asparagus in boiling salted water for about 5 minutes, then drain and dry with a kitchen towel.
2. Whisk the eggs in a large bowl along with chopped parsley, grated cheese, breadcrumbs, a pinch of salt, and ground pepper.
3. Heat a 24 cm omelette pan over moderate heat. Add the eggs and then add the asparagus. Allow the eggs to cook for a minute or two, then begin folding the uncooked runny eggs underneath with a spatula.
4. Flip the frittata in the pan, or place a plate over the pan and carefully turn over the pan, dropping the eggs onto the plate, and then sliding the eggs back into the pan.
5. Cook until the eggs are completely cooked and have turned lightly golden. Serve hot or cold.

Notes:

_____

_____

_____

_____

_____

_____

Cunigghiu 'cca pagghia

(Sweet and sour rabbit)

Ingredients (serves 4):

1kg rabbit, 4 florets cauliflower, 4 heads endive, 4 sticks celery, 1 small onion, 1 tsp tomato puree, 2 tbsp capers, 40 g raisins, 20 g pine nuts, ½ glass vinegar, 3 tbsp sugar, extra virgin olive oil, salt, pepper.

Preparation:

1. Clean cauliflower, celery, and endive. Drain and lightly fry them in a small amount of olive oil.
2. Cut the rabbit into portions and brown it in olive oil with salt and pepper. Add a few tablespoons of water, cover, and simmer for about 20 minutes, stirring regularly.
3. In another pan, brown the sliced onion. When it is golden, add the tomato puree and stir on moderate heat for a few minutes with a wooden spoon.
4. Add the rabbit pieces, the vegetables, capers, raisins, pine nuts, salt, pepper, and sugar. Stir until the sugar browns slightly, then add the vinegar and let it evaporate for a few minutes. If necessary, add a small amount of water. Serve hot or warm.

Notes:

_____

_____

_____

_____

_____

_____

Fassumauru

(Falso Magro – "fake lean")

Fassumauru is a Sicilian recipe that traces its origins back to the 1800s when French chefs, known as Monsú (from the French word Monsieurs), delighted their masters with a special dish called "Viande farcie de maigre" - stuffed lean beef roll.

In Sicily, where meat wasn't particularly popular, the Monsú had to get creative. They adapted their original recipe by enhancing the local tough meat with non-lean elements like salami, hard-boiled eggs, ham, and cheese.

The Sicilians, eager to imitate the rich and noble, unable to understand French, soon renamed this fusion French-Sicilian dish as Falso Magro: a truly original "Fake-Lean."

Ingredients:

700-800 g veal, 200 g prosciutto cotto (cooked ham), 4 hard-boiled eggs, 100 g smoked pancetta, 75 g ground beef, 1 fresh spring onion, 1 beaten egg, 1 garlic clove, 100 g caciocavallo or provolone diced, 60 g grated pecorino with peppercorn, 1 bunch of parsley, 100 g freshly shelled peas blanched in salted water, Tomato sauce, 1 walnut-sized chunk of butter (traditionally lard was used), Half a glass of red wine, Extra virgin olive oil, Salt, Pepper.

Preparation:

1. Pound the meat, keeping it rectangular in shape without puncturing it.
2. Lay slices of prosciutto cotto over the meat.
3. Arrange hard-boiled eggs lengthwise down the middle of the meat.

4. Trim the pancetta's rind, if necessary, place it around the eggs, then sprinkle diced cheese, parsley, minced garlic, and spring onion.
5. For the filling, combine ground meat, grated cheese, and peas. Spread the mixture over the other ingredients and roll the meat around it.
6. Tie the roll with string horizontally, vertically, and down (or used meat netting).
7. Brown the fassumauru in a mix of butter and oil in a large pan. Sprinkle it with red wine and continue cooking until the wine evaporates. Add tomato sauce diluted in water, and simmer the roll covered for about an hour, adding water if necessary.
8. When serving, transfer it to a platter, remove the string, and slice it into 1.5 cm slices.

Cathedral, Noto (Sr)

Liatina

(Aspic)

This traditional dish is a treasure from my family's Christmas celebrations. Here's the recipe:

Ingredients:

1 pig's ear, 2 pig's feet, 1 pig's knuckle.

For the broth:

Water, white vinegar, salt, lemon, red hot chili pepper.

Preparation:

1. Scrape and flame the pig, then soak the pieces in cold water for 12 hours.
2. Wash the pieces thoroughly and place them in a large saucepan.
3. Cover the pieces with a mixture of 4 parts water and 1 part vinegar. Add salt and slices of lemon.
4. Let it cook for 2 hours from when the liquid starts boiling.
5. Once the meat is well-cooked, remove it from the broth and set it aside. Separate the meat from the bones and store it in the fridge.
6. Filter the broth and let it cool until it coagulates.
7. Carefully remove the layer of fat formed on top and melt the aspic on the stove.
8. Cut the meat into pieces of at least 2 cm, place it on a plate with high edges, and pour some broth over it to cover the meat. Return it to the fridge.
9. As it continues to coagulate, add the remainder of the broth and the red chili pepper. Put it in the fridge again.

10. Once well coagulated, it is ready to be served in slices or cubes.

Notes:

_____

_____

_____

_____

_____

_____

Spiaggia dei Conigli (rabbits beach), Lampedusa

Puppetti 'cco sucu

(Meatballs with tomato sauce)

Ingredients:

½ kg minced veal or beef, 50 g breadcrumbs soaked in milk and squeezed dry, 25 g grated Parmesan cheese, 2 garlic cloves, 1 tbsp chopped parsley, 1 tsp finely grated lemon zest, 2 eggs, beaten, flour for coating, extra virgin olive oil for shallow frying, 300 ml tomato sauce, grated nutmeg, salt and pepper.

Preparation:

1. In a bowl, combine the breadcrumbs, meat, garlic, parsley, lemon rind, cheese, nutmeg, and salt and pepper to taste.
2. Add the beaten eggs and mix together lightly but thoroughly.
3. Gently shape tablespoonfuls of the mixture into golf ball shapes. Roll them lightly in flour and refrigerate until needed.
4. Heat oil in a large frying pan over moderate heat. When hot, add the meatballs in batches and fry for 3 to 4 minutes, turning until brown on all sides. Drain on paper towels.
5. Add the tomato sauce to the pan, thinning it to a pouring consistency with water if necessary.
6. Return the meatballs to the pan, stir gently, and simmer for 15 to 20 minutes until cooked through.
7. Serve the meatballs with sauce over spaghetti, penne, or fusilli pasta.

Notes:

_____

_____

_____

_____

_____

_____

Ficutu frittu 'cc' acitu

(Sweet and sour liver)

Ingredients:

800 g this sliced liver, extra virgin olive oil, ½ glass vinegar, 3 tsp sugar, 3 garlic cloves, fresh mint, salt, pepper, flour to coat liver.

Preparation:

1. Dredge both sides of the sliced liver in flour and shake to remove the excess.
2. Heat oil and fry the liver on each side until done, making sure not to overcook it.
3. Set aside the fried liver on a serving dish and season with mint, salt, and pepper.
4. Brown the crushed garlic in olive oil, ensuring not to burn it. Remove from heat and carefully add vinegar and sugar.
5. Return to the heat and reduce the vinegar and sugar mixture for 2 minutes, then pour it on top of the liver.

Notes:

_____

_____

_____

_____

_____

_____

Sangeli o Sancunazzu

(Pig Black pudding)

Ingredients:

1 kg fresh pig's blood (talk with your butcher), 100 g walnut, almonds, pine nuts, 50 g raisins, powdered cinnamon, salt, black pepper, sausage casing.

Preparation:

1. Scald walnuts and almonds in boiling water, peel them, and lightly toast them in the oven. Let them cool and grind them with the pine nuts.
2. Whip the blood with a whisk and add the ground nuts, the raisins previously softened in hot water, salt, pepper, and a pinch of cinnamon.
3. Pour the mixture into a saucepan and put it on very low heat, stirring until the liquid is as thick as cream.
4. Pour the mixture into the casing, sealed on one side with a string, then seal the other side.
5. Put in boiling water for about 10 minutes.
6. Drain it and serve in 1 cm slices.

Notes:

_____

_____

_____

_____

_____

_____

Ficateddi ri pollu

(Chicken livers)

Ingredients (serves 4):

500 g chicken livers, 2 medium onions, extra virgin olive oil, 1 tbsp vinegar, salt, black pepper, 2 tbsp tomato puree, 1 bunch parsley, ½ glass red wine.

Preparation:

1. In a skillet, heat olive oil over medium heat. Add the finely sliced onion, and cook until translucent.
2. Add the chicken livers and sauté until lightly browned, about 5 minutes.
3. Add the tomato puree, the wine, and sauté over medium-high heat for 3 or 4 minutes. Add the balsamic vinegar.
4. Let the mixture boil for another 2-3 minutes. If needed, add a bit of hot water. Lower the heat and let the mixture simmer for 15 minutes.
5. Season, to taste, with salt and pepper. Remove from the heat. Add the parsley and mix through.
6. Serve hot with some slices of toasted bread.

Notes:

_____

_____

_____

_____

_____

_____

Stigghiole

(Lamb bowel roasted)

This is a typical dish from Palermo. "Stigghiole" are the intestines of lamb, smoked over the grill. They are typically washed in water and salt, grilled with parsley and served with salt and lemon.

Ingredients:

Lamb bowel, 2 bunches parsley with long stems, lemon, salt, pepper, spring onion (optional).

Preparation:

1. Wash the inside and outside of the bowel and rub it with lemon.
2. Roll it tight around 5 or 6 stems of parsley and the spring onion.
3. Put these rolls on the barbecue after you have salted them.

Notes:

_____

_____

_____

_____

_____

_____

Myths and Legends

The legend of the Baroness of Carini

Based on a real historical event, there is a fascinating legend about ghosts that tells us about a famous baroness who lived in Carini in the 1500s and whose name was Laura Lanza. At the age of 14, she was forced by her father to marry Don Vincenzo la Grua Talamanca, Baron of Carini, a village in the province of Palermo.

After some time, she was disappointed because she had hoped to live happily with the baron. On the contrary, he left her alone most of the day to take care of his lands. So, she fell in love with her husband's cousin, Ludovico Vernagallo, and they became lovers. Eventually, the husband discovered the love story of the baroness, and Laura and Ludovico were murdered in the castle.

Her father, Cesare Lanza, Count of Trabia, wrote to Philip II of Spain confessing to the killing in a letter, but her husband was also suspected on account of rumours that he planned to marry again. This letter is still preserved in the Cathedral in Carini.

Nowadays, it is possible to visit the castle and also the famous 'murder room' where the baroness, fatally struck by her father, left the blood-stained imprint of her hand on the wall.

In February 2010, police in Sicily called in an international team of forensic scientists and criminologists to help solve the case of the murdered Baroness, 447 years after the crime. The investigation coincided with a project to rebuild parts of Carini Castle that have collapsed over time.

The crime scene has recently been restored, and a red handprint has been painted on the wall to mark the spot where, legend has it, the struggling Baroness left a bloody imprint, which reappears every year to mark the anniversary of her murder, on the night of December 4th, while the restless ghost of Laura wanders in the castle.

Castle of Carini, Palermo

Trippa alivitana

(Tripe Olivetana style)

The church of Saint John of the Hermits is one of the most famous destinations in Palermo. Originally, it was a monastery where the nuns were used to preparing this tripe dish called "Olivetana".

Ingredients (serves 6)

2 kg par-cooked tripe, 2 bay leaves, 2 garlic cloves, whole skin of ½ lemon, 1 small eggplant, oil to fry, 4 tbsp extra virgin olive oil, 1 onion, 1 small envelope of saffron, salt, pepper, 2 eggs, grated, pecorino cheese, parsley.

Preparation:

1. Cut the tripe into strips, about 4x2 cm, and place in a pot with an abundant amount of lightly salted water with the bay leaves, and bring to a boil.
2. Cook for 25 minutes, remove from the pot using a slotted spoon, and place in a colander to drain. Discard bay leaves.
3. Fry the eggplant cut into 1 cm thick slices and set aside.
4. In a large skillet, heat olive oil over low heat, add onions and when translucent, turn the heat up to medium, add tripe and sauté for 5 minutes.
5. Dilute the saffron in 100 ml of water and add to the pot. The cooking tripe should be soupy; if it is too dry, add more water, taste for salt and pepper, simmer for a few minutes.
6. Whisk the eggs with 2 tablespoons of grated cheese and as the tripe is simmering rapidly, blend in the eggs-cheese mixture and as soon as the eggs coagulate, remove from the stove and serve.

7. Garnish each dish with some of the fried eggplant and freshly chopped parsley.

Staircase of Saint Maria of the Mountain, Caltagirone

Involtini alla siciliana

(Stuffed roll of meat Sicilian style)

Ingredients:

800 g veal loin, sliced extra virgin olive oil, 1 finely chopped onion, 60 g lightly toasted breadcrumbs, 60 g finely grated pecorino cheese, 60 g softened raisins, 40 g pine nuts, chopped parsley, the finely grated zest of 1 lemon, salt, black pepper, fresh bay leaves.

Preparation:

1. In a small skillet, heat 2 tablespoons of the olive oil on medium-high heat and sauté the onion until tender and translucent.
2. Transfer to a small mixing bowl and add the breadcrumbs, cheese, raisins, pine nuts, parsley, and lemon zest. Season with salt and pepper, to taste. Set aside for filling.
3. Drizzle the beef slices with 4 tablespoons of the remaining olive oil. Season with salt and pepper.
4. Divide the breadcrumb mixture evenly among the beef slices, about 2 tablespoons each.
5. Using your fingers, roll the slices lengthwise up and over the filling until the meat is completely rolled up. Using butcher's twine, tie each roll firmly to secure.
6. Thread the meat rolls onto 2 skewers, 1 at either end of the roll, and thread bay leaves and onions onto each skewer, then top with a second beef roll and 2 more onions, until you have used all of the ingredients, like a kabob. Lightly brush each skewer with some of the remaining olive oil.

7. Grill the skewers, turning occasionally, about 4 to 5 minutes per side. Set skewers aside to rest for 5 to 10 minutes before serving.

Notes:

_____

_____

_____

_____

_____

_____

Trippa 'cco sucu

(Tripe Stewed with Tomato)

Ingredients (serves 4):

2 kg par-cooked tripe, 2 bay leaves, extra virgin olive oil, 1 onion, 1 tbsp tomato puree, 1 stalk of celery, 1 carrot, 1 can of peeled tomatoes (800 g), basil leaves, salt, pepper, grated pecorino cheese, 350 g cooked sweet peas.

Preparation:

1. Cut the tripe into strips, about 4x2 cm, and place in a pot with an abundant amount of lightly salted water with the bay leaves. Bring to a boil and cook for 25 minutes.
2. Remove from the pot using a slotted spoon and place in a colander to drain. Discard bay leaves.
3. Drain and set aside the liquid from the peeled tomatoes. Cut the tomatoes into pieces and set aside with the tomato juice.
4. In a large skillet, heat olive oil over low heat. Add onions, celery, and carrots and cook for about 5 minutes. Add the tomato puree diluted in 100 ml of water and cook for an additional 5 minutes.
5. Add the tripe to the pot, sauté for 5 minutes, and add the peeled tomatoes, salt, and pepper.
6. Simmer for 25 minutes, correct for salt and pepper, and continue cooking until the tripe is tender.
7. Add cooked peas, bring to a boil, and serve immediately.

Notes:

_____

_____

_____

_____

_____

_____

Fish

Cathedral, Cefalú

View of Sambuca di Sicilia, Agrigento

Sarde a beccafico

(Beccafico style Sardines)

Beccafico (figpecker) is a little bird similar to a warbler or quail. These little birds are so named because they like to peck figs. In the past, French chefs called 'monsù' used to prepare an elaborate dish based on these birds for the Sicilian aristocracy because their meat was really nice and tender. Once again, people imitated that recipe, replacing the birds with the more common and affordable sardines. Beccafico-style Sardines are very common in Palermo and Catania food shops and restaurants, representing one of the most typical dishes of Sicilian cuisine. Sarde a beccafico are generally served as an antipasto.

Ingredients (serves 4 to 6):

1 kg sardines, 1 diced onion, 150 g of toasted breadcrumbs, 4 chopped anchovy fillets, juice of 2 lemons, 2 tbsp of sugar, extra virgin olive oil, 50 g pine nuts, 50 g softened up raisins, chopped parsley, salt, pepper, bay leaves, 1 large slices of onion for each sardine.

Preparation:

1. Cut off the head of the sardines. In a large basin with cold water, immerse sardines, and scale them under water (to avoid a big mess).
2. Discard interior and by inserting the finger under the bone, eliminate it. Open the sardines leaving the two sides connected and the tail intact. Wash and drain.
3. Sauté the onions in olive oil, and after 7 minutes, add breadcrumbs. Cook for 2 minutes and set aside in a large bowl.

4. When breadcrumbs cool off, add the juice of 1 lemon, 1 tablespoon of sugar, fillets of anchovies, pine nuts, raisins, and parsley. Add salt and pepper to taste.

5. Gently pat dry the sardine fillets with paper towels, place 1 tablespoon of breadcrumb on the large side of the fillet (opposite the tail), fold and roll up, and arrange stuffed sardines in the oiled pan, tail up.

6. Alternate a slice of onion and a bay leaf between each Sarda a Beccafico.

7. Whisk the remaining olive oil with lemon and sugar, and sprinkle over sardines, shake leftover breadcrumb mixture on top.

8. Bake for 15 minutes at 400 degrees. Serve hot or at room temperature. Garnish with sliced lemon.

Baccalà 'a Missinisa

(Stockfish Messina stile)

Ingredients:

800 g salt cod – soaked in water for at least 36 hours, 1 chopped onion, extra virgin olive oil for sautéing, 2 garlic cloves, 250 g tomatoes peeled, seeded and chopped, 2 tbsp tomato paste diluted in 120 ml hot water, 60 g pitted black olives, 1 tbsp capers, 800 g potatoes cut into cubes, 1 medium-hot red pepper, salt to taste.

Preparation:

1. In a pan, heat a small amount of olive oil and sauté the onion over medium heat until soft and beginning to colour. Add the garlic and sauté for a couple of minutes more.
2. Add the tomatoes, tomato paste diluted in water, olives, and capers. Cover and simmer for about 10 minutes over low heat.
3. Meanwhile, cut the baccalà into 3 or 4 cm chunks and add them to the vegetables along with a cup of water (or half a glass of white wine). Let it simmer for an additional 30 minutes.
4. Add the potatoes and more water if necessary. Continue to simmer until the potatoes reach the desired tenderness.

Notes:

_____

_____

_____

_____

_____

_____

'Nzalata ri tunnu, patati, e aulivi

(Tuna, potato, and olives salad)

Ingredients:

180 g can of tuna in olive oil, 2 large potatoes, 8 ripe cherry tomatoes, 2 tbsp capers, 60 g pitted black olives, oregano, 2 garlic cloves, parsley, 2 tbsp white wine vinegar, extra virgin olive oil, salt, black pepper.

Preparation:

1. Boil the potatoes for around 30 minutes until they are cooked through but still firm. Slice the cherry tomatoes in half and set aside.
2. To make the dressing, finely chop the garlic and mix it in a bowl with the capers, dried oregano, olives, vinegar, and olive oil.
3. Remove the potatoes from the pot and allow them to cool just enough to handle, then peel them while they are still warm. Cut them into 3-4 cm pieces and place them in a salad bowl.
4. Break apart the tuna meat and add it to the bowl with the potatoes, then add the sliced tomatoes. Season with salt and pepper to taste. Pour the dressing over the salad and toss. Add the chopped parsley, and if desired, more olive oil and vinegar. Serve immediately.

Notes:

_____

_____

_____

_____

_____

Myths and Legends

The Cyclopes and Polyphemus

Children of Uranus and Gaia, they were four monstrous giants – Bronte, Sterope, Arge, and Polyphemus - each with a single eye in the middle of the forehead. They manufactured the lightnings of Zeus (Jupiter) in the workshops on Mount Etna.

In Homer's Odyssey (Book 9), Odysseus lands in proximity to the volcano where the Cyclopes were living, during his journey home from the Trojan War. The story is well-known. Polyphemus kills and eats six of Odysseus's fellows. The desperate Odysseus devises a clever escape plan, offering Polyphemus a strong wine that makes him drunk.

When Polyphemus asks for Odysseus' name, he tells him "μή τις," literally "nobody." As the Cyclops falls asleep, the Greek hero blinds him with a sharp club.

Polyphemus yells for help from his fellow Cyclopes that "nobody" has hurt him. The other Cyclopes think Polyphemus is making a fool out of them, and they grumble and go away. In the morning, Odysseus and his men escape from the cave by tying themselves to the undersides of Polyphemus' sheep.

Polyphemus tries to sink them by throwing big stones into the sea, but he misses them because of his blindness. These rocks are believed to be the Faraglioni of Acitrezza and Acicastello.

Faraglioni, Aci Trezza (Ct)

Murruzzu 'a matalotta

(Codfish matalotta style)

Ingredients (serves 4):

4 fresh cod fillets, 12 ripe cherry tomatoes, 50 g pitted Sicilian green olives, 1 tbsp capers, 2 garlic cloves, oregano, extra virgin olive oil, chilli pepper, salt, ½ glass white wine, hot water.

Preparation:

1. Wash and clean the cod fillets. Dry them with kitchen paper, dredge them in flour, and place them in hot oil. Cook until opaque on both sides and set aside.
2. Heat a large pan over moderate heat with olive oil. Toss the garlic cloves, scatter olives and capers in the pan, and stir until they're sizzling. Pour in the crushed tomatoes and half a glass of white wine, and after a couple of minutes, add 2 or 3 cups of hot water.
3. Turn up the heat, correct the salt, and partially cover the pan. After 10 minutes, lay the cod fillets in the pan in one layer, and pour in any fish juices that accumulated in the platter. Shake the pan occasionally to distribute the sauce and slosh it over the fish.
4. When the cod is tender and the sauce is slightly thickened and flavourful, turn off the heat. Taste and adjust the seasoning. Just before serving, drizzle a tablespoon or two of olive oil over it and sprinkle parsley all over the top. Serve hot.

Notes:

_____

_____

_____

_____

_____

_____

Pisci spada 'a Ghiotta

(Swordfish ghiotta style)

Ingredients:

1 kg swordfish, 1 onion, celery stalk, 2 garlic cloves, 2 tbsp capers, pitted green olives, 2 tbsp softened raisins, 4 large ripe tomatoes, extra virgin olive oil, salt, flour for dredging.

Preparation:

1. Chop the onion and celery into small pieces. Rinse the capers under cold water. Cut the tomatoes in half and squeeze out the seeds, then chop them.

2. Dredge the swordfish in flour, covering it well. Heat 2 tablespoons of olive oil in a deep pan over moderate heat and fry the swordfish on both sides until nicely browned. Remove from the pan and set aside.

3. Keep the pan on the hob, lower the heat, and add enough olive oil to coat the bottom of the pan. Place the celery, onions, and garlic cloves in the pan and cook for a few minutes before adding the capers, olives, and raisins.

4. When the vegetables become lightly brown, stir in the chopped tomatoes, salt to taste, and cook for about five minutes. Put the swordfish in the pan, spoon some sauce over it, then cover and simmer.

5. After five minutes, turn over the swordfish, spoon more sauce on top, and cook for another five minutes or until the fish is thoroughly cooked.

Notes:

_____

_____

_____

_____

_____

_____

Spiedini ri pisci spada

(Swordfish Kebabs Sicilian Style)

Ingredients (Serves 4):

800 g thinly sliced swordfish, 150 g dried breadcrumbs, extra virgin olive oil, salt, pepper, chopped parsley, capers, Parmesan cheese, onion.

Preparation:

1. Delicately flatten the slices of swordfish with a meat mallet and cut them in half.
2. Season the dried breadcrumbs with salt, pepper, and chopped parsley.
3. Take three-quarters of the breadcrumb mixture and add minced capers and grated Parmesan, sprinkling with a little olive oil. Spoon this flavourful mixture onto the slices of swordfish, roll them up, and thread them onto a skewer, alternating the rolls with a quarter of an onion.
4. Moisten the skewers with olive oil and coat them with the remaining breadcrumbs.
5. Grill the "spiedini," turning them only once, on charcoal or in a very hot oven for a few minutes. Serve hot.

Notes:

_____

_____

_____

_____

_____

_____

Cernia 'a Matalotta

(Fillet of Grouper Matalotta Style)

This dish is a testament to the enduring influence of French domination; the Sicilian term "Matalotta" derives from the French word "matelot," meaning sailor.

Ingredients:

2 pounds skinless grouper fillet, flour for dredging, 4 garlic cloves, celery, pitted green olives, 2 ripe tomatoes, crushed by hand, extra virgin olive oil, parsley, capers, salt, chili pepper, white wine, hot water.

Preparation:

1. Slice the grouper fillet into evenly sized chunks, dredge them in flour, and sauté in hot oil until opaque on both sides. Set aside.
2. In the same pan, toss garlic cloves and chopped celery, season with chili pepper and ¼ teaspoon salt. Stir for a couple of minutes until the vegetables sizzle.
3. Add olives and capers to the pan, stirring until they sizzle as well. Pour in the crushed tomatoes and half a glass of white wine, followed by 2 or 3 cups of hot water. Turn up the heat, correct the salt, and partially cover the pan.
4. After 10 minutes, arrange the grouper chunks in the pan in a single layer, pouring in any fish juices from the platter. Ensure the chunks are nearly covered by the sauce; add more hot water if needed. Shake the pan occasionally to distribute the sauce and coat the fish.
5. Once the grouper is tender and the sauce has slightly thickened, turn off the heat. Taste and adjust the seasoning. Just before

216

serving, drizzle a tablespoon or two of olive oil and sprinkle parsley over the top. Serve hot.

Notes:

_____

_____

_____

_____

_____

Zuppa ri cozzi

(Mussels soup)

Ingredients:

1 kg mussels, 1 onion, finely diced, 8 garlic cloves, 4 lightly crushed and 4 minced, ½ glass white wine, 12 ripe cherry tomatoes, halved, 1 bunch of parsley, chopped, basil leaves, red chili pepper, to taste, extra virgin olive oil, salt to taste, black pepper, freshly ground.

Preparation:

1. Wash and scrub the mussels thoroughly, removing the beards.
2. In a large pot over high heat, add ½ glass of olive oil, diced onions, and at least 4 lightly crushed garlic cloves. Cook for a few minutes, ensuring not to burn the garlic.
3. Pour in the white wine, add halved tomatoes, fresh ground black pepper, and a pinch of chili pepper. Then, gently introduce the mussels to the pot.
4. Cover and steam for approximately 15 minutes, stirring the bottom shells occasionally to ensure even cooking.
5. Once the mussels are cooked, add the minced garlic and chopped parsley. Give it a good stir.
6. Ladle the mussel soup into serving bowls, garnish with basil leaves, and serve alongside slices of toasted bread.

Notes:

_____

_____

_____

_____

_____

_____

Calamari cini

(Filled squids)

Ingredients:

800 g cleaned squid, 3 minced garlic cloves, minced parsley, minced celery, minced onion, 100 g breadcrumbs, raisins, pine nuts, tinned peeled tomatoes, extra virgin olive oil, salt, pepper.

Preparation:

1. Remove the tentacles from the squid and keep the bodies whole.
2. In a pan, sauté minced onion, celery, and garlic in half of the olive oil until softened.
3. Chop the tentacles finely and add them to the pan. Sauté for a few minutes and set aside.
4. In a bowl add raisins, pine nuts, parsley, and breadcrumbs and the cooked tentacles. Season with salt and pepper, and mix well.
5. Stuff the squid bodies with the prepared mixture, but avoid overfilling to prevent splitting during cooking. Secure the openings with toothpicks.
6. In a heavy pot, sauté the stuffed squid on all sides with a little olive oil until browned.
7. In a separate large pan, brown garlic, then add peeled tomatoes. Let the sauce cook for 10 minutes, adjusting the salt.
8. Place the stuffed squid into the pan with the tomato sauce and cook for an additional 20 minutes.
9. Serve hot, generously topped with the flavourful tomato sauce.

Notes:

_____

_____

_____

_____

_____

_____

Tunnina Ca Cipuddata

(Tuna with Onions)

This delightful fresh tuna recipe from Eastern Sicily is perfect for serving approximately 6 people. Its versatility makes it an excellent choice for warm summer months, and the fact that it can be prepared in advance adds to its appeal.

Ingredients:

1 kg fresh ventresca di tonno (tuna cut from the underside of the fish), or use available tuna cut into 2 cm slices, 200 g finely sliced onions, flour, parsley, white wine, vinegar, extra virgin olive oil, salt, black pepper.

Preparation:

1. Flour the slices of tuna, sprinkle with salt, and fry them in oil until golden, turning carefully for even cooking (about 9-10 minutes for a 2 cm thick piece, 4-5 minutes per side).
2. Remove the fish and replace the oil. Slowly cook the onions in the pan, ensuring they don't overcook (add a little water if needed).
3. Once the onions are soft and creamy, generously sprinkle them with strong vinegar. Return the fish to the skillet.
4. Sprinkle minced parsley over the dish, season with black pepper to taste, and give it a final sprinkle of vinegar.
5. The dish is ready to be enjoyed hot or cold.

Notes:

_____

_____

_____

_____

_____

_____

_____

'Nzalata ri puppu

(Octopus Salad)

Ingredients (serves 4):

2 kg octopus, cleaned and boiled, 1 ½ kg potatoes, peeled and cut into medium dice, 2 stalks of celery, cut into julienne, 3 carrots, cut into julienne, 150 g black pitted olives, 1 tbsp white wine vinegar, juice of 3 lemons, parsley, extra virgin olive oil, black pepper, salt.

How to Boil the Octopus:

Tenderize the octopus by dipping it three times into hot water for 10 seconds each time. Boil the octopus for about 1 hour and let it cool in the cooking water. Cut it into large pieces.

Preparation:

1. Bring a pot of water to a boil, add 1 tablespoon of vinegar, a handful of salt, and boil the potatoes for 10-15 minutes.
2. In a large bowl, combine abundant olive oil, salt, parsley, black pepper, and lemon juice. Whisk the dressing until homogeneous.
3. Place the octopus in hot water for about 1 minute, then drain. Also, drain the potatoes and transfer them to the bowl with the dressing.
4. Add olives, celery, and carrots. Toss together until all ingredients are well coated.
5. Transfer the salad to a serving plate, pour more dressing, sprinkle with parsley, and drizzle with olive oil. Better served lukewarm.

Notes:

_____

_____

_____

_____

_____

_____

Baccalà 'a matalotta

(Salted Codfish marinara style)

Ingredients (serves 4):

600 g codfish, desalinated, 500 g potatoes, 1 spring onion, 30 g capers, 2 ripe tomatoes, 50 g black olives, 1 garlic clove, 1 bunch of parsley, extra virgin olive oil, salt, black pepper, white wine.

Preparation:

1. Heat a large pan over moderate heat with olive oil.
2. Toss in garlic cloves, strew olives, and capers into the pan. Stir until they're sizzling.
3. Pour in crushed tomatoes, add a layer of sliced potatoes, half a glass of white wine, and 2 or 3 glasses of hot water after a couple of minutes. Turn up the heat, correct the salt, and partially cover the pan.
4. Place the boned and cut codfish on top of the potatoes and cook over low heat.
5. Pour half a glass of white wine and cook for about half an hour.

Notes:

_____

_____

_____

_____

_____

_____

Concordia Temple, Temples Valley, Agrigento

Places & Traditions

Marsala and its wine

The town of Marsala, on the southwestern coast of Sicily, is well-known worldwide for the aromatic wine that bears its name. The most credible version of the introduction of Marsala fortified wine to a wider range of consumers is attributed to the English trader John Woodhouse.

In 1773, Woodhouse landed at the port of Marsala and discovered the local wine produced in the region, aged in wooden casks and tasting similar to the Spanish and Portuguese fortified wines then popular in England.

Fortified Marsala wine was, and still is, made using a process called in perpetuum, similar to the solera system used to produce Sherry in Jerez, Spain. Woodhouse recognized that the in perpetuum process raised the alcohol level and alcoholic taste of this wine while also preserving these characteristics during long-distance sea travel.

Woodhouse further believed that fortified Marsala wine would be popular in England. Marsala wine indeed proved so successful that Woodhouse returned to Sicily, and in 1796, began the mass production and commercialization of Marsala wine.

Marsala is crafted from local, indigenous white grapes—like Catarratto, Grillo (the most sought-after grape for Marsala production), or the highly aromatic Inzolia grape. The ruby-coloured Marsala hails from any combination of three local red grape varietals.

The fermentation of Marsala is halted by the addition of grape brandy when the residual sugar content reaches predetermined levels according to the sweet/dry style the maker is aiming for. Similar to the solera system of blending various vintages of Sherry, Marsala often goes through a perpetuum system, where a series of vintage blending takes place.

Desserts

Crema ri ricotta

(Ricotta cream)

The ricotta cream is widely used in Sicilian desserts as a filling for cannoli, cassate, crispelle, sfingi, and various other pastries. The rich taste of this mixture also makes it a dessert to serve alone, dressed with chocolate chips or caramelized sugar.

Ingredients (serves 8):

1 kg ricotta, 250 g icing sugar, zest of 1 orange, 3 pinches of cinnamon powder, 1 drop of vanilla essence.

Preparation:

Mix the ricotta and sugar well in a large bowl until smooth. Blend in the zest of the orange, cinnamon powder, and the vanilla essence, and store in the fridge for a few hours. Before using it, mix the ricotta cream with a wooden spoon to make it silky-smooth.

To create a visually appealing dessert, sprinkle a dessert dish with icing sugar. Place a generous spoon of ricotta cream and sprinkle with crushed pistachios. Finish the plate with some chocolate cream drops.

Notes:

_____

_____

_____

_____

_____

_____

233

Sfinci ri patati

(Potatoes Doughnuts)

Ingredients:

300 g finest flour, 200 g potatoes, 2 eggs, 10 g yeast, 1 lemon, sugar, milk, cinnamon, extra virgin olive oil.

Preparation:

1. Peel potatoes and boil them in salted water.
2. Mash the boiled potatoes and add flour, yeast (dissolved with two tablespoons of sugar in a small amount of warm milk), eggs, 5 tablespoons of oil, and the grated zest of the lemon.
3. Add a small amount of warm milk and work the mixture into a soft dough that should easily detach itself from the work surface.
4. Leave the dough to rise until it doubles in volume.
5. Roll small amounts between your thumb and forefinger to make rings.
6. Deep fry each ring one by one on moderate heat until they swell up and turn golden brown.
7. Place the fried rings on absorbent paper to remove excess oil.
8. Sprinkle the rings generously with sugar and powdered cinnamon.

Notes:

_____

_____

_____

_____

_____

_____

Biancu mangiari

(Almond jelly)

Ingredients:

150 g whole almonds (preferably peeled), 150 g sugar, 12 g gelatine sheets (unflavoured), 250 ml cream, 250 ml water, 2 tablespoons orange blossom water.

Preparation:

1. Prepare the gelatine by soaking it in a bowl of water.
2. If the almonds are not peeled, blanch them in boiling water for 1 minute to easily remove the skins. Strain and drain them on a cloth.
3. Place the perfectly white almonds in a food processor with a small amount of water until coarsely ground. Add the rest of the water until it becomes a thick liquid.
4. Strain and squeeze the almond mixture in a clean, dry cloth over a bowl to separate the almond milk from the almond meal. Discard the almond meal.
5. In a saucepan, combine the almond milk with cream, sugar, and orange blossom water. Add the drained gelatine.
6. Carefully bring the mixture to a boil and let it simmer for a couple of minutes. Remove from heat.
7. Pour the mixture into ramekins and let them cool. Refrigerate for four hours.
8. To serve, warm the ramekins slightly by dipping them in hot water or using a damp cloth. Tip them upside down onto dishes and sprinkle chopped almonds on top.

Notes:

_____

_____

_____

_____

_____

_____

237

Cannola 'cca ricotta

(Cannoli with ricotta)

Ingredients:

250 g plain flour, 1 tsp cocoa powder, 1 tsp freshly ground coffee, 30 g softened butter, 25 g sugar, 60 ml white wine, 1 beaten egg, olive oil for deep-frying, icing sugar to decorate.

For the filling:

600 g ricotta cheese, 150 g icing sugar, 25 g chocolate chips, 50 g candied fruits, finely chopped.

Preparation:

1. Make the filling by whisking ricotta and icing sugar in a large bowl until creamy. Fold in the chocolate chips and finely chopped candied fruits. Set aside.
2. Prepare the pastry mixing flour, cocoa powder, coffee, butter, and sugar in a large bowl. Gradually add the wine and mix until the mixture forms pastry dough. Form the pastry into a ball and wrap it in cling film. Let it rest for an hour.
3. Lightly flour a clean work surface and roll out the pastry to a thickness of about 3 mm. Using a round pastry cutter, cut circles with a diameter of about 7.5 cm and wrap them around tubular moulds, securing the edges with the beaten egg.
4. Heat olive oil in a large pan to 180°C. Fry the cannoli until golden-brown. Drain on paper towels and gently remove the moulds.
5. Let them cool, then fill the cannoli with the ricotta mixture. Sprinkle with icing sugar and serve.

Notes:

_____

_____

_____

_____

_____

_____

Cava Grande Ponds, Avola

Cassata Siciliana

(Sicilian Cassata)

The genesis of Sicilian cassata may very well be traced to the Arab era, or shortly afterward to the Arab-influenced kitchens of Norman-Sicilian monasteries, as a very simple concoction of eggs and flour. After some centuries of evolution, it is today a richly decorated baroque cake of aristocratic proportions. The foundation of cassata is an egg cake known as "pan di Spagna"—referred to by the English misnomer "sponge cake." You could buy one or you can prepare it by following the instructions in this recipe. It is sprinkled with a sweet liqueur such as Maraschino cherry and orange flower water and has a filling made from strained fresh ricotta mixed with sugar, pistachios, cinnamon, candied fruits, and chocolate. Baroque decorations are added using sugar icing and coloured candied fruits, apricot preserves, apricot jelly, and marzipan delights such as miniature pears, cherries, kumquats, and slices of candied citron twisted into bows, curlicues, or rosettes.

Ingredients:

For the Sponge Cake (22-inch cake tin):

3 large whole eggs, 3 large egg yolks, 160 g granulated sugar, 70 g all-purpose flour, 95 g potato starch, grated zest of 1 lemon (or grated zest of orange), 1 packet of vanilla sugar (or vanilla extract), a pinch of salt.

For Ricotta and Chocolate Cream:

800 g well-drained ricotta (ideally from sheep), 300 g granulated sugar, 150 g dark chocolate chips, 50 g high-quality candied orange peel (optional).

200 g of ready-made marzipan or for "Pasta Reale":

300 g almond flour, 300 g sugar, 75 g water, green powdered food colouring.

Sugar glaze for Cassata:

about 350 g of vanilla-flavoured icing sugar (but you may need more), warm water.

Icing for decoration:

75 g of vanilla-flavoured icing sugar, 2 drops of fresh lemon juice, 1egg white.

For the finishing touch:

Mixed candied fruit (candied oranges, candied citron, cherries).

Preparation:

For the sponge cake:

1. Whip together, at maximum speed, the eggs all together with the sugar, finely grated lemon zest, a pinch of salt, and vanilla.
2. We should obtain a very clear, frothy, very dense, and compact mixture that quadruples in volume.
3. This step is important so that the eggs incorporate air and give the final volume to our sponge cake without the addition of leavening agents.
4. Then add the sifted flour and potato starch gradually and in several steps. Mix slowly by hand from the bottom upwards with a wooden spoon or spatula to avoid deflating the dough and achieve a frothy and airy mixture.
5. Pour the batter into a previously buttered and floured baking pan and bake in a preheated oven at 180°C for about 35 minutes. Do not open the oven for at least 30 minutes. When a golden crust forms on the surface, check with a toothpick—it should come out dry!

6. Remove from the oven, let it cool for 15 minutes in the pan. Loosen the sides of the cake with a knife, open the pan, and let it cool on a cake rack.

For Ricotta Cream:

1. Take the fresh ricotta, place it in a clean kitchen towel, and let it rest until you obtain completely dry ricotta! Completely dry ricotta is essential for the success of the cassata.
2. When the ricotta is dry, place it in a bowl with the sugar, and work it with a spoon. Then blend everything with a hand blender. This method will allow you to obtain a smooth and velvety mixture in a few seconds without sifting. Then add the chocolate chips, mix with a spoon, and refrigerate. Do not cover with plastic wrap to avoid condensation, at most use a clean kitchen towel.

For the Marzipan (or use ready-made marzipan):

1. Place the water in a high-sided pot and heat it on the stove. Add the sugar previously mixed with the food colouring and let it dissolve completely, stirring continuously until you see bubbles.
2. Remove from the heat and add the almond flour, mix well. Pour the mixture onto a work surface and let it cool by kneading for 6-10 minutes, dusting with a little powdered sugar if it sticks. The marzipan should be smooth and velvety.
3. Shape it into a ball, seal it in plastic wrap, and let it rest in the fridge (at least 3 hours before using it).

Assemble the Cassata

1. Roll out the marzipan with a rolling pin to a thickness of 4 mm. Dust the cake tin with powdered sugar and line it with the marzipan, taking care that it adheres perfectly. Trim the edges with a knife.

2. Brush the edges and lightly the bottom of the sponge cake with sugar water or water flavoured with rum or maraschino. Do not moisten too much.

3. Finally, pour the cold and perfectly compact ricotta cream and chocolate drops. Leave 1 cm from the edge and then place the last circle of sponge cake, also cut to size to fit the edge of the pan.

4. This last disc will be the bottom of the cassata and must remain dry. Seal with cling film and refrigerate for a few hours. Flip the cassata onto a large dessert plate and put it back in the fridge.

Icing for Cassata:

1. To prepare the icing for the Sicilian cassata, place half of the sugar in a bowl and start mixing with 1 teaspoon of warm water. You should obtain a soft icing that drips from the spoon, not too hard, but not excessively soft either.

2. To achieve the right consistency, add warm water one teaspoon at a time. Pour it over the cassata covering all of it. Spread it evenly with the help of a spatula also on the sides.

3. Return the cassata in the fridge for another 1h.

For the decoration, use your imagination to create designs with the candied fruits. For example, you can place a candied half mandarin in the centre of the cassata and arrange the candied fruits around it to create the shape of leaves.

The final touch will be given by the decoration with royal icing, which you will prepare by beating an egg white until stiff and gradually adding powdered sugar until you achieve a very dense consistency. With a pastry bag equipped with a nozzle with a rather thin hole, create decorations both on the top and on the edges of the cassata to make it even richer and more sumptuous.

Notes:

_____

_____

_____

_____

_____

_____

Vinu cottu

(Cooked Wine)

Cooked wine can be used as a sweet condiment, as well as being sparingly drizzled over strongly flavoured foods such as game, roast meats, poultry, or aged cheeses.

Ingredients:

Must (freshly pressed juice of grapes before fermentation), fresh orange peels, cinnamon stick.

Preparation:

1. In a heavy stainless steel pot, cook the must over low heat, simmering until it is reduced by half. Cover and leave it in the same pot to cool overnight.
2. The next day, add some orange peels and a ¼ stick of cinnamon, return to low heat, simmer, and reduce by half.
3. Cool and filter the cooked wine, then store it in clean glass bottles or jars, making sure they are tightly sealed.

Notes:

_____

_____

_____

_____

_____

_____

Cubbaita o Giuggiulena

(Sesame nougat)

Cubbaita, or Giuggiulena is an old nougat version developed by the Arabs who lived in Sicily.

Ingredients:

500 g honey, 230 g sugar, 450 g sesame seeds, 230 g blanched, peeled, minced almonds, orange or lemon zest.

Preparation:

1. Grease with oil a shallow pan or a piece of marble to pour the cooked confection. In a 3 quart sauce pan mix all ingredients.
2. Cook over a medium flame, stirring continuously between 5 to 10 minutes until sugar caramelizes (at 250 to 275 degrees, if you have a candy thermometer) and mixture becomes lightly golden. Don't burn the mixture, keep an eye on it.
3. Pour mixture in the greased pan or on the marble counter and with the help of a greased spatula level the nougat and shape it into a uniform block, about 1 cm thick. Before it gets cold cut into 3x6 cm pieces.
4. Wrap and seal each piece in wax paper and the giuggiulena will keep if properly stored in an airtight container.

Notes:

_____

_____

_____

_____

_____

_____

Alcantara Gorge, Motta Camastra

Turruni ri mennula

(Almond nougat)

Ingredients:

1 kg toasted almonds, 500 g honey, 500 g caster sugar, orange zest, cinnamon.

Preparation:

In a saucepan, melt the honey over low heat and gradually add the sugar, mixing well until it caramelizes.

Add the almonds, mix well, and incorporate the cinnamon and orange zest, both cut into small pieces.

Stir everything for a couple of minutes, then pour the almond nougat onto a surface covered with sugar and roll it out with an oiled wooden rolling pin.

Cut it into pieces before the nougat cools down and wrap each piece in parchment paper once it's cold.

Notes:

_____

_____

_____

_____

_____

_____

Pignolata

(Messina pignolata)

Typical sweet dating back to the period of Spanish domination in Sicily, widespread throughout the Messina area and in Reggio Calabria. Traditionally, the glazed "pignolata" was among the many sweets prepared exclusively between Christmas and Carnival.

Ingredients:

500 g of 00 flour, 10-12 egg yolks, 67 ml of pure alcohol for desserts, vermouth, or another strong liquor like rum, 50 g of sugar, lard for frying as needed.

For the Chocolate Glaze:

200 g powdered sugar, 200 g unsweetened cocoa, 100 g butter, water as needed, vanilla as needed, cinnamon powder as needed.

For the Lemon Glaze:

300 g powdered sugar, juice of 3 lemons, 3 egg whites.

Preparation of the dough:

1. In a bowl, beat the egg yolks, sugar, and alcohol with electric beaters at high speed. Gradually add the flour, mixing until you obtain a homogeneous and consistent dough that tends to detach from the sides of the bowl.
2. Let it rest for a few hours, then roll out the dough on a floured surface, forming sticks about 7-10 mm thick. Cut the sticks into small pieces, each about a couple of centimetres long.

3. Fry the pieces of "pignolata" a few at a time in plenty of hot lard, turning them occasionally until they are lightly golden. Finally, place them on absorbent paper to drain excess fat.

For the chocolate glaze:

Melt the butter in a saucepan over very low heat. Gradually add the powdered sugar, vanilla, powdered cinnamon, sifted cocoa, and water. Pour the water slowly until you achieve the right consistency. Let it cool slightly.

For the lemon glaze:

Pour the sugar into a saucepan and heat it over very low heat until it starts to melt. Then, pour it into a bowl and gradually incorporate the beaten egg whites. Stir for a long time with a spoon, meanwhile pouring the lemon juice slowly, until you obtain a soft and white glaze.

Assembly of the pignolata:

Separate the previously fried pieces into two equal portions and mix the first portion well with the warm chocolate glaze and the second portion with the lemon glaze.

Arrange the two glazed portions of pignolata on a serving plate, side by side, to form a single two-coloured mound, or in smaller piles, always half for each glaze, and let the glazes dry for at least an hour.

Notes:

_____

_____

_____

_____

_____

_____

Myths and Legends

Arethusa (Siracusa)

Arethusa ("The Waterer") was a nymph and daughter of Nereus, making her a Nereid. She became a fountain on the island of Ortygia in Syracuse, on the East coast of Sicily.

The myth of her transformation begins when she encounters a clear stream and starts bathing, unaware that it is the river god Alpheus. He falls in love during their encounter, but she flees upon discovering his presence and intentions, as she wishes to remain a chaste attendant of Artemis.

After a long chase, she prays to her goddess for protection. Artemis hides her in a cloud, but Alpheus persists. She begins to perspire profusely from fear and soon transforms into a stream.

Artemis then breaks the ground, allowing Arethusa another attempt to flee. Her stream travels under the earth to the island of Ortygia, but Alpheus flows through the sea to reach her and mingle with her waters. The mixing of their waters creates this enchanted fountain surrounded by papyrus.

During Demeter's search for her daughter Persephone, Arethusa entreats Demeter to discontinue her punishment of Sicily for her daughter's disappearance. She tells the goddess that while traveling in her stream below the earth, she saw her daughter looking sad as the queen of Hades.

Arethusa occasionally appears on coins as a young girl with a net in her hair and dolphins around her head. These coins were common around Ortygia, the location where she ends up after fleeing from Alpheus. This legend was born to explain the presence of a freshwater fountain near the "salt" sea.

Fonte Arethusa, Siracusa

Savoiardi

(Lady Fingers)

Ingredients:

6 eggs, 150g sugar, 150g all-purpose flour, salt, icing sugar.

Preparation:

1. Separate the eggs. Whisk the egg yolks with half of the sugar and all of the vanilla. Beat until very light-coloured; this will take about 5 minutes.
2. In a clean bowl, beat the egg whites until they hold soft peaks. While beating, slowly add the salt and the remaining sugar until combined. Gently fold the beaten egg whites into the egg yolk mixture.
3. Sift the flour over the egg mixture and gently fold it in.
4. Fill the pastry bag with half of the batter and pipe 3 1/2-inch fingers, 1 1/2 inches apart, in rows on the parchment paper. Continue with the second half of the batter in the same manner.
5. Bake at 375 degrees F (190 degrees C) for about 15 minutes until firm to the touch and golden. Remove the paper and fingers from the baking sheet and place them on racks to cool.
6. After cooling, remove fingers from the paper and sprinkle icing sugar on top.

Notes:

_____

_____

_____

_____

_____

_____

Cuccìa ri Santa Lucia

(Cooked Wheat)

Cuccìa is a boiled wheat dessert usually mixed with ricotta cream, candied fruit, and chocolate shavings. It is a traditional sweet for the Feast of Saint Lucy on December 13, primarily prepared in Syracuse and Palermo.

Ingredients:

800 g ricotta (traditionally sheep's milk ricotta), 500 g soft wheat, 300 g sugar, 100 g chocolate chips, 100 g candied fruit, cinnamon powder to taste, one teaspoon of salt, a pinch of baking soda, water as needed.

Preparation:

For the ricotta cream:

Place the ricotta in a colander to drain and refrigerate until it has lost the whey, then sieve it, mix it well in a bowl with sugar, and add chocolate drops and candied fruit.

For cooking wheat:

After checking and cleaning it from any impurities, soak the wheat in water for three days, remembering to change the water every 24 hours.

After the three days of soaking, rinse the wheat under running water and boil it in plenty of water with a pinch of salt and a teaspoon of baking soda. It is recommended to cook it in a pressure cooker for about 50 minutes or extend the cooking time for at least three hours.

When the wheat has become swollen and very soft, let it cool in its cooking water, then drain it and season it with the ricotta cream and powdered cinnamon.

Notes:

_____

_____

_____

_____

_____

_____

Affucaparrini

(Strozzapreti biscuits)

Ingredients (Makes about 30 Biscuits):

600 g flour, 70 g sugar, 5 large eggs, pinch of salt, juice of 1 lemon, flour for dusting, water.

Preparation:

1. Make a well with the flour, place sugar, eggs, salt, and lemon juice in it, and combine. Mix the ingredients, adding some water if needed. Keep kneading until the mixture is smooth.
2. On a well-floured board, cut the dough into 2 pieces, and each piece into 2 parts. Knead the dough to make it compact and shape each piece into an elongated roll 1.5 cm in diameter. Cut it into 8 pieces and roll each piece into an S shape or small rings. Place each piece into a floured pan.
3. Bring a large pot of water to a boil and immerse the biscuits, a few at a time, into the boiling water. Using a slotted spoon, remove them as soon as the water starts to boil again.
4. Place the biscuits in pans and cover them with clean kitchen towels. Store them in a cool place for 24 hours.
5. Place the biscuits on baking paper, setting them 5 cm apart. Bake at 190 C degrees for about 15 minutes, until the cookies are a light golden colour. Serve the Affucaparrina with wine, preferably a sweet wine like Marsala, Moscato, or Passito.

Notes:

_____

_____

_____

_____

_____

_____

'Mpanatigghi

(Modica sweets)

It is said that 'mpanatigghi were made for the first time by monastery sisters moved to pity by the exhaustion of some brother preachers moving around monasteries during Lent. To help them, the sisters hid minced veal in the crushed almonds and chocolate pastries that they were allowed to consume during fasting periods.

Ingredients for the filling:

1 kg veal, finely minced, 1 kg sugar, 1 kg almonds, toasted and ground, 200 g dark chocolate, cinnamon, 12 egg whites.

Ingredients for the dough:

1 kg white flour, 300 g sugar, 300 g lard, 12 egg yolks, icing sugar.

Preparation:

1. Mix together flour, yolks, sugar, and melted lard. Knead by hand, mixing well. Spread some flour on a surface and roll out the dough in small pieces with a rolling pin until you have 6 cm round shapes.
2. Separately, place on the heat for a couple of minutes a pan with the minced veal, sugar, almonds, chocolate, cinnamon, and egg whites, stirring frequently.
3. Switch off the heat and put the filling into the round dough. Close the dough so that a half-moon shape will be obtained and make a cut in the top. Put in a hot oven at 180°C for 15 min. Serve the biscuits cold with icing sugar on top.

Notes:

_____

_____

_____

_____

_____

_____

Viscotta 'ri mennula

(Almond biscuits)

Ingredients:

300 g blanched almonds, 100 g sugar, grated zest of 1 lemon, 2 egg whites, salt, 1/2 teaspoon almond extract, 1/2 teaspoon vanilla extract, 30 whole blanched almonds, pine nuts, or candied cherries.

Preparation:

1. Working in batches, combine the blanched nuts with some of the sugar in a food processor. Process until finely ground. Transfer to a large bowl, add the rest of the sugar and the lemon zest, and combine well.
2. Beat the egg whites with a pinch of salt and the almond and vanilla extracts until stiff but not dry.
3. Add the egg white mixture to the almond mixture and stir lightly, not flattening the egg whites.
4. Pinch off enough dough to form a 2.5 cm ball. Flatten the balls very slightly, and place them 2.5 cm apart on a baking sheet.
5. Insert a whole almond or pine nut, pointed end up, or a candied cherry in the centre of each cookie.
6. Bake in a preheated oven, at 180 C until the cookies are lightly browned and have small cracks on the surface, 25 to 30 minutes.
7. Let cool briefly on the pan, then transfer to wire racks to cool completely.

Notes:

_____

_____

_____

_____

_____

_____

'Nfigghiulata

(Focaccia with ricotta cheese)

Ingredients:

For the dough:

500 g hard wheat flour, 1 tsp salt, 25 g brewer's yeast, 1 glass warm water, 2 tbsp olive oil. Pour the flour giving it a basin shape.

For the filling:

500 g ricotta cheese, Sugar, 1 egg, cinnamon.

Preparation:

1. Dissolve the yeast in a bit of warm water and pour it in the middle and then add the remaining water with the salt and start kneading.
2. Work well and for a long period of time the dough, and add the oil a bit per time. Cover the dough with flour and cover with a clean tablecloth. Let it rise in a lukewarm place for at least 30 min.
3. Whisk the ricotta and add egg, cinnamon, and sugar to taste until you achieve the desired sweetness.
4. Make a disk from the dough with a rolling pin and place it in an oiled tin.
5. Pour the ricotta over the dough and put another dough disk on top, sealing the edges.
6. Make two cross cuts in the centre and reverse the corners.
7. Put it in a hot oven for about 45 minutes.

It is possible to prepare smaller pastries with the same filling as shown in the picture below. Just make a disk of dough of 10 cm and put the filling in the middle. With the fingers, make 7 or 8 corners, merging the edges to obtain a cup shape.

Notes:

_____

_____

_____

_____

_____

_____

Viscotta a Esse

(S shaped Biscuits)

Ingredients:

500 g flour, 130 g sugar, 250 g unsalted butter (at room temperature), 4 egg yolks, ½ teaspoon baking powder, pinch of salt, 6 drops of vanilla, egg whites for washing.

Preparation:

1. Make a well with the flour, place sugar and butter in it, and combine.
2. Add eggs, salt, baking powder, and vanilla. Mix all ingredients, and then, using your hands, knead to bring the dough together.
3. Do not overmix. Do not handle the dough more than necessary. Refrigerate the dough for 1 hour.
4. Prepare a pan covered with baking paper.
5. Cut the dough into 4 pieces, and each piece into 2 parts. Knead the dough to make each piece compact and shape each part into a 1.5 cm roll. Cut it into 4 pieces, and with each piece, form small sticks about 10 cm long and 1.5 cm thick. Place each piece into the pan 4 cm apart and shape it to form an "S".
6. Beat some egg white, add 1 tablespoon of water and a pinch of salt, and use it for the egg wash.
7. With the help of a brush, go over the cookies with the egg wash and bake at 190 C degrees for 25 minutes or until the cookies are a golden colour.

Notes:

_____

_____

_____

_____

_____

_____

Piazza Duomo, Siracusa

272

Made in the USA
Monee, IL
11 November 2024

69811499R00157